AUTISM IN ADULT WOMEN

Empowering Women with Autism to Reach Their Full Potential

By

ODESSA WINFIELD

PREFACE

It all began with a simple question. One that seemed innocent enough but would soon open a door I had never thought to walk through. I had spent years immersed in the world of autism, particularly how it presents in adult women. I had read countless articles, sifted through piles of research, and written about the topic extensively. Yet, somehow, all of that knowledge felt distant—clinical even. The stories I'd shared were real, but they belonged to someone else. Until I met Rachel.

Rachel was not just another case study or a statistic in the ever-growing field of autism research. She was a woman, much like you and me, living in a world that often seemed to misunderstand and overlook her. She had reached out to me after reading a book I wrote earlier, thanking me for what she called "a glimpse of recognition in a sea of invisibility." Her words were powerful, and they stuck with me. We exchanged emails and then phone calls, and I was struck by how raw and honest she was about her experiences. Rachel didn't dress things up; she spoke about the daily realities of living with autism in a way that cut through the jargon and theories that often surround the condition.

So, when Rachel's usual caregiver had to leave abruptly due to a family emergency, she asked if I could step in. At first, I hesitated. I wasn't a professional caregiver, just a writer and a researcher. What did I know about the day-to-day realities of caring for someone on the spectrum? But Rachel, with her characteristic bluntness, simply said, "I don't need someone perfect. I just need someone who's willing."

It was that willingness that brought me to her door on a rainy afternoon, my suitcase in hand, and a head full of doubts. Rachel lived in a small, tidy apartment, surrounded by books, plants, and an almost intimidating array of sensory aids—noise-canceling headphones, fidget toys, weighted blankets. I knew, from my research, why she had these things, but seeing them arranged so meticulously was different. It made me realize how every part of Rachel's world had been carefully constructed to help her go the a reality that didn't always make sense.

Rachel welcomed me with a wary smile. I could sense her anxiety immediately. It radiated from her like heat, and I wondered if mine was equally palpable. She wasn't what I had pictured in my mind. She was younger, taller, with bright red hair that seemed to have a life of its own. She laughed more easily than I'd expected, but she also seemed to pull back just as quickly, as if worried she'd done or said the wrong thing. I quickly learned that she often felt that way—unsure of whether her words landed as she intended.

Those first few days were awkward. I found myself constantly second-guessing my actions. Was I talking too much? Too little? Did I make enough eye contact? Too much? I wanted so badly to do it right, to be the understanding, empathetic caregiver she needed, but I felt like I was always stumbling. Rachel was patient, but she also didn't shy away from calling me out when I misstepped. "You don't have to pretend to understand everything," she told me one evening after I had tried (and failed) to make her favorite tea correctly. "I'd rather you ask me a thousand questions than assume you know what I need."

I quickly learned that caregiving was about much more than just "helping" someone. It was about listening—really listening—and being prepared to leave behind everything I thought I knew. I was humbled by how much I had to unlearn. Rachel's needs were complex and ever-changing. Some days she needed quiet; other days, she needed to talk for hours about the intricate details of her favorite books or the scientific papers she was reading. Some mornings were filled with laughter and shared jokes, while others were lost in the fog of her anxiety or shutdowns. I began to see how much effort she put into masking—trying to fit into a world that didn't quite fit her.

One of the most powerful moments came in our second week together. Rachel had had a difficult day. She had ventured out to a local store, a task that seemed simple enough, but something had gone wrong—a conversation with a cashier that didn't go as she'd expected. When she returned, she was visibly agitated, her hands fluttering and her speech faster, almost breathless. I wanted to help, to comfort her, but I didn't know how. I asked if she wanted to talk about it. She shook her head and retreated to her room.

I remember standing outside her door, feeling utterly helpless. All my research, all my writing, seemed irrelevant at that moment. I didn't know what she needed. So, I waited. And waited. Finally, she emerged, quieter, still anxious, but calmer. She looked at me and said, "Sometimes, it's just too much. The noise, the people, the expectations. I can't always explain why. But it's like… everything is too bright, too loud, too close. And I just need space."

Her words hit me with a clarity I hadn't experienced before. I realized that so much of what I had been taught about autism was through a narrow lens—an academic one, a medical one, but not a lived one. Rachel's description was so visceral, so real. I realized then that I didn't need to have all the answers; I just needed to be there, to respect her process, and to create a space where she felt safe to express herself.

As the weeks passed, I saw Rachel's courage in a new light. She had spent a lifetime going through a world that often felt alien to her. I saw how she pushed herself to engage in social situations, even when every fiber of her being screamed against it. I watched as she carefully managed her sensory inputs, balancing her need for stimulation with her need for calm. She showed me that living with autism wasn't about overcoming a condition; it was about understanding and embracing a different way of experiencing the world.

Rachel also taught me the importance of celebrating small victories. Like the day she managed to call and schedule her own doctor's appointment—a task that had always overwhelmed her with anxiety. Or the afternoon she baked cookies, not because she particularly wanted cookies, but because it was an exercise in following a sequence, a skill she was working to strengthen. Each of these moments was a triumph, a reminder that progress doesn't always look the same for everyone.

There were, of course, difficult moments. Days when Rachel's anxiety was so high that she couldn't leave her room, or when sensory overload triggered meltdowns that left us both exhausted. During these times, I felt like I was failing her, that I wasn't doing enough. But Rachel, ever perceptive, would often remind me that it wasn't about "fixing" her or making everything better. "I'm not broken," she would say, "I just need things to be different sometimes."

That was perhaps the most significant lesson I learned during my time with Rachel—that there is no single way to live, no universal standard we must all adhere to. Her life, with all its unique challenges and joys, was no less valuable or worthy than mine. In fact, it was through her that I began to see the richness of neurodiversity, the different ways in which people can experience and interpret the world. Rachel taught me that there is a beauty in difference, a depth in the way she approached life that I had never fully appreciated before.

Over time, I stopped trying to be the perfect caregiver and started being a better listener. I began to understand that what Rachel needed most was not someone who had all the answers, but someone who was willing to walk alongside her, to ask questions, to make mistakes, and to learn from them. I started to see the nuances in her communication—the small changes in her tone of voice, the way her body language shifted when she was overwhelmed, or the quiet, focused intensity she brought to tasks that mattered to her. I learned to celebrate these subtleties, recognizing them as a part of who she was, rather than something that needed to be "managed" or "corrected."

I also started to see the limitations of the systems that were supposed to support people like Rachel. From healthcare to social services, it became painfully clear how ill-equipped many of these systems were to meet the needs of autistic adults, particularly women. I remember a particularly frustrating day when Rachel had an appointment with a new doctor. Despite the notes in her file and the detailed explanations we had prepared in advance, the doctor spoke to her as if she were a child, not an intelligent, articulate adult. Rachel, to her credit, remained composed throughout, but I could see the frustration and hurt in her eyes. Later, at home, she simply said, "Why is it so hard for people to see me for who I am?"

That question haunted me. It was a question that echoed throughout the stories of so many autistic women I had interviewed or read about over the years—women who felt unseen, misunderstood, and undervalued. Women whose strengths were often overlooked because they didn't fit the mold of what society expected or understood. My time with Rachel made that question feel more urgent, more pressing. It wasn't just a theoretical issue to be debated or analyzed; it was a lived reality, and it demanded attention.

As the days turned into weeks, and the weeks into months, I realized that I wasn't just there to care for Rachel—she was caring for me too, in ways I hadn't anticipated. She taught me patience and the value of slowing down in a world that often glorifies speed and productivity. She reminded me that connection isn't always about words or grand gestures; sometimes it's found in the quiet moments, the shared silences, or the simple act of being present. She showed me that vulnerability isn't a weakness, but a profound strength, a willingness to be seen as you truly are, with all your imperfections and fears.

Rachel and I didn't always agree. There were moments of tension, misunderstandings, and clashes of perspective. I remember one particular evening when I tried to push her to join a social group for autistic adults, believing it would be beneficial for her. She pushed back hard, telling me that I was projecting my own need for social connection onto her. "I'm fine as I am," she said. "I don't need to be more social to be more 'normal.'" That conversation made me confront my own biases and assumptions, to recognize the ways in which I was still unconsciously measuring her against a neurotypical standard.

It was humbling, to say the least. It forced me to let go of my preconceived notions and truly listen to what she wanted, rather than what I thought she needed. That shift in perspective changed everything. I started to see Rachel as she saw herself—a woman who was fiercely independent, who knew her own mind, who had dreams and desires that didn't always align with the mainstream. And that was okay. More than okay, it was beautiful.

When it was finally time for me to leave, I felt a deep sense of gratitude but also a profound sadness. I had come to care for Rachel deeply, not just as someone with autism, but as a friend, a teacher, and a remarkable human being. She had opened my eyes to a world I thought I knew but had only glimpsed from a distance. She had challenged me, frustrated me, taught me, and ultimately transformed me.

I left Rachel's home with a heavy heart, but also with a renewed sense of purpose. I realized that my role as a writer, as an advocate, was not just to share information or raise awareness, but to amplify voices like Rachel's—to tell their stories, in their own words, to the world. I wanted to bring to light the complexities, the joys, the struggles, and the triumphs of autistic women in a way that was real and raw and honest.

This book is deeply influenced by my time with Rachel. It is a reimagining of what it means to write about autism in adult women. I have tried to move beyond the clinical and the academic to capture the lived experiences, the voices, and the stories of the women themselves. I want this book to be a space where autistic women can see themselves reflected, where they can find understanding, support, and, most importantly, community.

To the readers of this book, whether you are autistic yourself, a family member, a friend, a caregiver, or simply someone seeking to learn, I hope that Rachel's story, and the stories of so many other women like her, resonate with you. I hope it challenges you to think differently, to see differently, and to approach the world with a little more empathy, understanding, and openness.

This book is not a definitive guide or an all-encompassing answer. It is a collection of experiences, of voices, of lives lived on the margins and in the center, in silence and in sound, in solitude and in community. It is a celebration of neurodiversity and a call to action—a call to listen, to learn, to advocate, and to create a world where every woman, autistic or not, can live her life fully, authentically, and unapologetically.

And to Rachel, thank you for sharing your world with me. Thank you for your patience, your honesty, and your courage. You have taught me more than any book, any study, or any research ever could. You have shown me the true meaning of what it is to be seen, to be heard, and to be valued for exactly who you are. This book is dedicated to you and to all the women who continue to fight for their voices to be heard and their stories to be told.

May we all learn to listen a little better. May we all learn to see a little clearer. And may we all strive to create a world where every woman, in all her diversity, feels truly at home.

With gratitude,
Odessa Winfield

TABLE OF CONTENTS

INTRODUCTION

When I first began writing about autism, I quickly noticed a glaring omission in the existing literature: the voices and stories of autistic adult women. In a world where the understanding of autism has long been shaped by the experiences of young boys and men, countless women have been left out of the narrative—often misunderstood, misdiagnosed, or entirely overlooked. This book exists to help change that.

But why this book, and why now? Because autistic adult women deserve to be heard, understood, and supported. You deserve a resource that speaks directly to you—one that acknowledges your unique experiences, challenges, and triumphs. Too often, autistic women find themselves on the fringes of the conversation, struggling to see themselves reflected in the existing knowledge about autism. Many of you have shared with me stories of late diagnoses, years of feeling different but not knowing why, and a deep yearning for understanding that goes beyond the stereotypes and assumptions.

This book is here to fill that gap. It's not just about providing information; it's about offering validation, comfort, and empowerment. It's about creating a space where you can see yourself fully—where your strengths are recognized, your struggles are understood, and your experiences are valued. This book aims to be a companion on your journey, whether you are just discovering your autistic identity, navigating the complexities of adulthood, or seeking a deeper understanding of yourself.

I also wrote this book for those who love and support autistic women—partners, friends, family members, and allies who want to understand better and advocate more effectively. This is a guide to empathy and action, a call to see beyond the surface, and an invitation to join a conversation that has been too quiet for too long.

....

Understanding autism in adult women begins with acknowledging that it often looks different from what the world has come to expect. The diagnostic criteria historically developed around young boys don't always capture the nuanced reality of autistic women. Many women on the spectrum have spent their lives adapting, masking, and camouflaging their traits to fit in. This isn't due to a lack of authenticity or honesty; it's often a survival strategy in a world that doesn't always make space for difference.

This can mean that your experiences as an autistic woman might not match what you've read or been told about autism. Maybe you've struggled with social dynamics in ways that aren't immediately visible to others. Perhaps you've always felt deeply overwhelmed by sensory inputs—bright lights, loud noises, scratchy fabrics—but have been told you're just "too sensitive." You might have found yourself exhausted by the effort of "passing" as neurotypical, feeling like you're performing a role that was never meant for you.

Autistic women often experience what is known as "masking"—a phenomenon where they learn to suppress their autistic traits to blend into neurotypical society. While this can help you navigate social situations, it often comes at a significant personal cost. Masking can lead to burnout, anxiety, depression, and a sense of disconnection from one's true self. This book will help you understand the impact of masking and provide strategies to unmask in a way that feels safe and empowering.

....

One of the most profound challenges for autistic women is navigating a world that was not built with your needs in mind. The neurotypical world is filled with unspoken social rules, sensory minefields, and expectations that can feel impossible to meet. This book will guide you through some of the most common challenges, from finding and maintaining meaningful relationships to thriving in a work environment that may not understand or accommodate your needs.

We'll look into practical strategies for daily living, such as managing executive functioning challenges, organizing your time, and creating routines that support your well-being. We will also explore the sensory sensitivities that many autistic women experience—how to recognize your triggers, advocate for yourself, and create environments where you can feel comfortable and safe.

But navigating the neurotypical world is not just about coping or surviving. It's about finding ways to live authentically and joyfully. It's about understanding that your unique perspective is valuable and that you have the right to exist in the world as you are—not as someone else wants you to be. You don't have to apologize for your differences; you can celebrate them, and this book will help you do that.

How to Use This Book

This book is designed to be a comprehensive guide and a companion on your journey. You can read it cover to cover, or you can jump to the sections that resonate most with where you are right now. Each chapter is structured to provide both understanding and action—offering insights into the experiences of autistic women, as well as practical tips and strategies you can apply in your daily life.

This book is an invitation to pause, think, and connect with yourself in new ways. They are designed to help you discover what works for you—what brings you peace, joy, and a sense of belonging.

This book is not a one-size-fits-all solution. It recognizes that every autistic woman is unique, with her own strengths, challenges, and ways of being in the world. It is here to offer guidance, but also to encourage you to trust your own instincts and knowledge. You are the expert on your own life, and this book is here to support you in owning that expertise.

So, welcome to this journey. Whether you are newly diagnosed or have known you are autistic for years, whether you are seeking support for yourself or trying to better understand someone you love, this book is for you. It is an invitation to explore, learn, and grow. It is a celebration of the richness and diversity of autistic women's lives.

I hope that as you read, you will feel seen, understood, and empowered. I hope you find comfort in these pages and that they help you discover new ways to navigate the world that honor your true self. Above all, I hope this book becomes a trusted friend, one you can turn to whenever you need guidance, support, or simply the reassurance that you are not alone.

CHAPTER 1

UNDERSTANDING AUTISM

Autism Spectrum Disorder (ASD): A Brief Overview

Autism Spectrum Disorder, or ASD, is a developmental condition that affects how a person communicates, interacts with others, and experiences the world around them. The term "spectrum" is key here because it highlights the diversity within autism—no two autistic individuals are exactly alike. Some people may need significant support in their daily lives, while others may require little to no assistance. Understanding this spectrum is the first step in grasping what autism truly is.

When we talk about autism, we're referring to a set of traits and behaviors that can manifest in different ways. These traits usually appear in early childhood, though they might not be fully recognized until later, especially in cases where the traits are less obvious. The core characteristics of autism typically revolve around three main areas: social communication, repetitive behaviors, and restricted interests.

Social communication challenges are often what people first notice in someone with autism. This might include difficulty with eye contact, understanding body language, or interpreting social cues. For instance, an autistic person might not automatically know when it's their turn to speak in a conversation, or they might find it hard to understand jokes or sarcasm. This doesn't mean they don't want to communicate; rather, they might do so in ways that are different from what others expect.

Repetitive behaviors and restricted interests are another hallmark of autism. These can take many forms, from repetitive movements like hand-flapping or rocking, to a deep fascination with specific topics or hobbies. For some, these behaviors are comforting or help them make sense of their environment. It's important to recognize that these behaviors are not inherently negative—rather, they are part of what makes each autistic person unique.

The exact causes of autism are not fully understood, though research suggests a combination of genetic and environmental factors. What is clear is that autism is not caused by bad parenting or vaccinations—an important point to remember, as we'll discuss further in the myths and misconceptions section. Autism is a lifelong condition, but with the right support, autistic individuals can lead fulfilling lives.

One crucial aspect of understanding autism is recognizing the diversity within the spectrum. Some autistic individuals might have co-occurring conditions, such as anxiety, ADHD, or epilepsy, which can affect their experiences and the support they need. Additionally, each person's strengths and challenges can vary widely. For example, while one person might excel in logical thinking and problem-solving, another might have exceptional creativity or attention to detail.

The way autism is perceived has evolved significantly over the years. In the past, autistic individuals were often misunderstood or marginalized, leading to a lack of appropriate support and opportunities. Today, there is greater awareness and appreciation of neurodiversity—the idea that neurological differences like autism are natural variations of the human experience, rather than deficits or disorders to be "fixed."

However, despite this progress, challenges remain. Autistic individuals often face societal barriers, such as stigma, discrimination, and a lack of understanding. This can make everyday activities, such as going to school, finding a job, or forming relationships, more difficult. But with increased awareness and acceptance, these barriers can be reduced, allowing autistic individuals to thrive.

Understanding autism also involves recognizing the importance of early intervention and support. For children diagnosed with autism, early intervention can make a significant difference in their development and quality of life. This might include speech therapy, occupational therapy, or specialized educational programs. For adults, support might involve job coaching, social skills training, or access to mental health services.

Ultimately, understanding autism is about more than just recognizing the traits and behaviors associated with the condition. It's about appreciating the individuality of each autistic person and acknowledging their unique perspectives and contributions. It's about moving away from a one-size-fits-all approach and embracing a more personalized understanding of what it means to be autistic. By doing so, we can create a more inclusive and supportive society for everyone.

Common Myths and Misconceptions

Autism is a subject surrounded by many myths and misconceptions. These misunderstandings can lead to stigma, discrimination, and unnecessary challenges for autistic individuals and their families. It's important to debunk these myths to foster a more accurate and compassionate understanding of autism.

One common myth is that autism is caused by vaccines. This misconception gained traction in the late 1990s when a now-discredited study falsely linked the MMR vaccine (measles, mumps, and rubella) to autism. Numerous studies since then have thoroughly debunked this claim, finding no evidence to support a connection between vaccines and autism. The initial study was retracted, and its lead author lost his medical license. Despite this, the myth persists, leading some parents to avoid vaccinating their children, which can have serious public health consequences.

Another widespread misconception is that all autistic individuals have intellectual disabilities. While it's true that some autistic people may have co-occurring intellectual disabilities, many do not. Autism exists across all intellectual levels, and some autistic individuals have average or above-average intelligence. It's important to recognize that intelligence and autism are not inherently linked, and each person's abilities and challenges are unique.

A related myth is the idea that autistic people lack empathy. This is one of the most damaging misconceptions about autism. In reality, many autistic individuals experience emotions deeply and care a great deal about others, but they may express empathy in ways that are different from neurotypical expectations. For example, an autistic person might struggle to interpret someone's emotions based on facial expressions but feel intense concern and a desire to help when they learn someone is upset. Understanding this distinction is crucial in dispelling the myth that autistic people are "emotionless" or "cold."

There's also a myth that autism is a childhood condition and that people "grow out of it" as they get older. Autism is a lifelong condition, and while the way it manifests can change over time, it doesn't go away. Many autistic adults were either diagnosed late or not at all, leading to a lack of support throughout their lives. Recognizing that autism is present across the lifespan is important for ensuring that autistic individuals receive the support they need at all stages of life.

Another common myth is that all autistic people are savants, like the character in the movie "Rain Man." While it's true that some autistic individuals have extraordinary talents or abilities in specific areas, this is not the case for everyone. The savant stereotype can be harmful because it creates unrealistic expectations and can overshadow the everyday challenges that autistic people face. It's important to appreciate and support the individual strengths and needs of each autistic person, rather than expecting them to conform to a narrow stereotype.

A myth that often affects women is the belief that autism is a "male" condition. Historically, autism has been diagnosed more frequently in males, leading to the misconception that it's rare in females. However, research now shows that autism is underdiagnosed in women and girls, partly because they may present differently than males. This has led to many women being misdiagnosed or going undiagnosed until adulthood. Understanding that autism affects people of all genders is essential for ensuring that everyone receives the recognition and support they need.

The idea that autism is a "tragedy" or that autistic individuals are "suffering" from their condition is another harmful misconception. While autistic people may face challenges, especially due to societal barriers and a lack of understanding, many do not view their autism as a tragedy. In fact, many autistic individuals and advocates embrace neurodiversity and see autism as an integral part of their identity. This perspective emphasizes the need to focus on acceptance and support rather than pity or attempts to "cure" autism.

Another myth is that autism can be "cured." There is no cure for autism, nor is one needed. Autism is a neurodevelopmental condition that is part of who a person is. Efforts to "cure" autism often stem from a misunderstanding of what autism is and can be harmful to autistic individuals. Instead of seeking a cure, the focus should be on providing support, accommodations, and acceptance to help autistic people lead fulfilling lives.

It's also important to address the misconception that autistic people can't lead independent lives. While some autistic individuals may need significant support, others are fully capable of living independently, pursuing careers, and forming meaningful relationships. With the right support and accommodations, many autistic people can thrive in various aspects of life. It's crucial not to underestimate their potential based on stereotypes or assumptions.

By challenging and debunking these myths, we can move towards a more accurate and compassionate understanding of autism. This not only benefits autistic individuals and their families but also helps to create a more inclusive society where everyone is valued for who they are.

How Autism Presents Differently in Women

Autism has historically been seen as a predominantly male condition, but this perception is changing as more attention is given to how autism presents in women. The differences in how autism manifests in women compared to men can lead to underdiagnosis, misdiagnosis, and a lack of appropriate support for autistic women.

One of the key differences in how autism presents in women is the tendency for many autistic women to "mask" or "camouflage" their traits. Masking involves consciously or unconsciously hiding autistic behaviors and mimicking neurotypical behaviors to fit in socially. This might include forcing oneself to make eye contact, suppressing stimming behaviors (repetitive movements or sounds that can be soothing), or carefully imitating the social behaviors of peers. While masking can help autistic women navigate social situations, it can also be exhausting and lead to anxiety, burnout, and a loss of self-identity.

Because of this masking, the classic signs of autism may be less visible in women. For example, an autistic woman might appear socially adept on the surface, but underneath, she could be struggling with anxiety, sensory overload, or difficulty understanding social nuances. This can make it harder for others to recognize that she is autistic, leading to delays in diagnosis or misdiagnosis with conditions such as anxiety, depression, or borderline personality disorder.

Autistic women may also have different social interests and behaviors compared to autistic men. While boys on the spectrum might show a strong interest in topics like trains or computers, girls might be deeply interested in animals, literature, or social justice causes—interests that can be mistaken for typical gendered behaviors rather than signs of autism. Additionally, autistic girls and women might be more likely to engage in imaginative play or form intense friendships, which can mask their social challenges.

Another way autism can present differently in women is in the realm of sensory processing. Many autistic individuals experience heightened or reduced sensitivity to sensory stimuli, such as sounds, lights, textures, or smells. In women, these sensory sensitivities might manifest in specific ways, such as being overwhelmed by bright lights or loud noises, or having strong preferences for certain clothing materials. These sensitivities can impact daily life, but they might not always be recognized as part of autism, especially if they are not accompanied by other more visible autistic traits.

The differences in how autism presents in women also extend to emotional regulation. Autistic women might experience intense emotions but struggle to express them in ways that others understand. This can lead to misunderstandings or the perception that they are "overreacting" or "too sensitive." Additionally, the internalized pressure to conform to social expectations can lead to mental health challenges, such as anxiety, depression, or eating disorders, which are more common in autistic women than in autistic men.

It's also important to consider the impact of societal expectations and gender roles on how autism is perceived in women. Society often expects women to be more socially adept, nurturing, and communicative, which can lead to greater pressure on autistic women to mask their traits. This societal pressure can contribute to feelings of inadequacy or isolation, especially if they feel they are not meeting these expectations.

Furthermore, the underdiagnosis of autism in women can have significant consequences. Without a diagnosis, autistic women may struggle to understand why they find certain aspects of life difficult, leading to feelings of confusion or self-doubt. They may also miss out on crucial support and accommodations that could help them navigate challenges and build on their strengths. For those who receive a late diagnosis, there can be a mix of relief in finally understanding themselves and frustration at the lack of earlier recognition.

Despite these challenges, there is growing recognition of the unique ways autism can present in women, leading to more research, better diagnostic tools, and greater awareness among healthcare providers. Autistic women are also increasingly speaking out about their experiences, advocating for greater understanding and acceptance. This shift is helping to ensure that autistic women receive the recognition and support they need, allowing them to embrace their identities and lead fulfilling lives.

Understanding how autism presents differently in women is crucial not only for accurate diagnosis but also for providing appropriate support and accommodations. By recognizing the diversity within the autism spectrum and the specific ways it can manifest in women, we can move towards a more inclusive understanding of autism that benefits everyone.

Diagnosing Autism in Adulthood

For many individuals, receiving an autism diagnosis in adulthood can be a life-changing experience. It can bring clarity and understanding to a lifetime of feeling different, misunderstood, or out of sync with the world around them. However, the path to an adult autism diagnosis is often fraught with challenges, including misdiagnosis, societal misconceptions, and a lack of awareness among healthcare professionals.

One of the primary reasons many autistic individuals are not diagnosed until adulthood is that autism can present differently in adults compared to children. In children, the signs of autism are often more pronounced, such as delayed speech development, difficulties with social interaction, or repetitive behaviors. In adults, especially those who have developed coping mechanisms or who mask their autistic traits, these signs may be less obvious.

For women in particular, the journey to diagnosis can be even more complicated. As discussed earlier, many autistic women are adept at masking their traits, which can lead to their struggles being overlooked or misattributed to other conditions, such as anxiety or depression. Additionally, the diagnostic criteria for autism have historically been based on how the condition presents in males, leading to underdiagnosis in females. This has left many women navigating life without the understanding or support they need.

The process of diagnosing autism in adulthood typically begins with self-reflection or the suggestion from a loved one that certain traits might be indicative of autism. This might include difficulties with social interactions, sensory sensitivities, or a strong need for routine and predictability. Many adults who seek a diagnosis have often felt different or out of place for much of their lives, but they may not have recognized these feelings as being related to autism.

Once someone decides to pursue a diagnosis, the next step is usually to consult with a healthcare professional who specializes in autism. This might be a psychologist, psychiatrist, or neurologist with experience in diagnosing autism in adults. The diagnostic process often involves a thorough assessment, including a detailed personal history, observation of behaviors, and possibly standardized tests or questionnaires designed to identify autistic traits.

One of the challenges of diagnosing autism in adulthood is that many autistic adults have developed coping mechanisms that help them navigate the neurotypical world. These coping strategies can sometimes obscure the signs of autism, making it harder for healthcare professionals to recognize the condition. For example, an autistic adult might have learned to make eye contact or engage in small talk, even if these behaviors are uncomfortable or exhausting. It's important for healthcare providers to ask questions that delve deeper into the individual's experiences, rather than relying solely on surface-level observations.

For those who do receive a diagnosis in adulthood, the experience can be both validating and liberating. Finally having a name for their experiences can provide a sense of relief and a better understanding of why certain aspects of life have been challenging. It can also open the door to support, accommodations, and communities of others who share similar experiences.

However, receiving an adult autism diagnosis can also bring up complex emotions. Some individuals might feel anger or sadness about not being diagnosed earlier, especially if they have struggled for years without understanding why. Others might worry about the stigma or misconceptions associated with autism and how their diagnosis will be perceived by others. It's important for individuals in this situation to have access to support, whether through therapy, support groups, or online communities, where they can process these emotions and connect with others who have had similar experiences.

For some, an adult autism diagnosis can also lead to changes in how they approach various aspects of life, such as work, relationships, and self-care. Understanding their autistic traits can help individuals identify strategies for managing sensory sensitivities, social interactions, and stress. It can also empower them to advocate for their needs, whether in the workplace, in social situations, or in their personal lives.

It's also worth noting that not all autistic adults choose to pursue a formal diagnosis. Some may recognize their autistic traits and identify with the autism community without feeling the need for

an official label. Others might face
barriers to accessing a diagnosis, such as
financial constraints, lack of access to
specialized healthcare providers, or
concerns about the potential
consequences of being diagnosed. It's
important to respect each

CHAPTER 2

THE JOURNEY TO DIAGNOSES

Recognizing the Signs in Yourself or a Loved One

The journey to an autism diagnosis often begins with a moment of realization—an awareness that certain behaviors, challenges, or experiences don't quite align with what is typically expected. This moment might come gradually, as a series of observations build up over time, or it might be more sudden, prompted by something you read, a conversation you had, or a specific incident that made you question whether you or someone you love might be autistic.

Recognizing the signs of autism in yourself or a loved one is the first crucial step toward understanding and seeking a diagnosis. These signs can manifest in various ways, and they often differ between individuals. For many, the first indications are social difficulties. You might notice that you or your loved one struggles with understanding social cues, maintaining eye contact, or engaging in small talk. Social situations might feel overwhelming or confusing, leading to a preference for solitude or interactions with a small, trusted circle.

For others, sensory sensitivities might be the most noticeable sign. Everyday stimuli like bright lights, loud noises, or certain textures might be overwhelming or even painful. This heightened sensitivity can make environments like crowded shopping malls or noisy classrooms particularly challenging. On the other hand, some individuals might have a reduced sensitivity to stimuli, not noticing things like extreme temperatures or pain in the same way others do.

Another sign to look for is a strong need for routine and predictability. Many autistic individuals find comfort in having a structured daily routine and can become distressed when that routine is disrupted. This need for consistency can also extend to preferences for specific foods, clothing, or activities. Changes or unexpected events might cause significant anxiety or lead to a meltdown, which is an intense response to sensory overload or emotional stress.

Special interests are another hallmark of autism. These are intense, focused interests in specific topics or activities, often to the exclusion of other pursuits. You or your loved one might be able to spend hours researching a particular subject, collecting related items, or engaging in a favored hobby. These interests can bring great joy and satisfaction, but they might also be misunderstood by others who don't share the same level of enthusiasm.

Communication differences are also common. This might include difficulty with verbal communication, such as finding the right words, or a preference for nonverbal forms of communication. Some autistic individuals might have delayed speech development, while others might speak fluently but struggle with the nuances of conversation, such as understanding sarcasm or metaphor. It's also possible to have a literal interpretation of language, where phrases like "raining cats and dogs" are taken at face value.

You might also notice repetitive behaviors, such as hand-flapping, rocking, or repeating certain words or phrases. These behaviors, often referred to as "stimming," can be a way to self-soothe, manage anxiety, or express excitement. While these behaviors might seem unusual to those unfamiliar with autism, they are a natural part of how many autistic individuals regulate their emotions and sensory experiences.

If you're recognizing these signs in yourself or a loved one, it's important to remember that autism exists on a spectrum. This means that the traits can vary widely in how they present, and not everyone will exhibit every sign. Some people might have more subtle signs that are easy to overlook, especially if they've learned to mask or compensate for their differences over time. Masking, which involves hiding or suppressing autistic traits to fit in with societal expectations, is particularly common among women and can make it harder to recognize the signs of autism.

At this stage, it's natural to feel a mix of emotions. You might feel a sense of relief at finally understanding why certain things have always felt different or challenging. On the other hand, you might also feel overwhelmed, anxious, or uncertain about what this realization means. It's important to give yourself or your loved one the space and time to process these feelings. Remember that recognizing the signs is just the beginning of the journey, and seeking a diagnosis can be an empowering step toward greater self-understanding and support.

Overcoming the Barriers to Diagnosis

Seeking an autism diagnosis, especially in adulthood, can be a daunting process. There are several barriers that might stand in your way, from societal misconceptions and stigma to practical challenges like finding a knowledgeable healthcare provider. Understanding these barriers and knowing how to navigate them can help you or your loved one move forward on the path to diagnosis.

One of the most significant barriers is the pervasive stigma surrounding autism. Despite increasing awareness, many people still hold misconceptions about what it means to be autistic. This can lead to fears about being judged, misunderstood, or treated differently if you pursue a diagnosis. These concerns are especially prevalent among adults who may worry about how a diagnosis could impact their work, relationships, or self-image. It's important to remember that seeking a diagnosis is a personal decision, and it doesn't change who you are—it simply provides a framework for understanding your experiences and accessing the support you might need.

Another barrier is the internalized belief that you or your loved one might not "fit" the typical image of autism. This is particularly common among women, who are often underdiagnosed or misdiagnosed because the traditional diagnostic criteria were developed based on how autism presents in males. If you've spent years masking your traits or adapting to societal expectations, it might be hard to see yourself in the descriptions of autism that are commonly portrayed. However, it's important to recognize that autism is a spectrum, and there is no one way to be autistic. Trust your instincts if you feel that something doesn't quite add up, and don't be afraid to seek out more information or professional guidance.

Access to healthcare professionals who are knowledgeable about autism in adults is another significant challenge. Many healthcare providers are more familiar with diagnosing autism in children and might not recognize the signs in adults, especially if those signs are subtle or masked. It can be frustrating to encounter professionals who dismiss your concerns or attribute your experiences to other conditions, such as anxiety or depression. If this happens, don't be discouraged—consider seeking a second opinion or looking for a specialist who has experience with adult autism.

Financial barriers can also play a role. The process of getting a diagnosis can be expensive, especially if you need to see a specialist or if your insurance doesn't cover the necessary assessments. For some, the cost can be a major obstacle, leading them to delay or forgo seeking a diagnosis altogether. If you're facing financial barriers, it might be worth exploring community resources, sliding-scale clinics, or organizations that offer support for individuals seeking an autism diagnosis.

The diagnostic process itself can be another barrier. It often involves multiple appointments, assessments, and interviews, which can be time-consuming and emotionally draining. The process might also require you to revisit difficult or painful experiences from your past, which can be challenging. It's important to approach this process with patience and self-compassion, and to reach out for support if you need it. This could be from a trusted friend, family member, or therapist who understands what you're going through.

For those who are recognizing the signs in a loved one, especially in a child, there can be additional barriers related to acceptance and advocacy. It can be difficult to accept that your child might be autistic, especially if you weren't expecting it or if you have preconceived notions about what autism means. You might worry about their future, how they will be treated by others, or how you will manage the challenges that come with raising an autistic child. These feelings are natural, but it's important to move beyond them and focus on getting your child the support they need. Remember that early intervention can make a significant difference in your child's development and quality of life.

Advocating for a diagnosis can also be challenging, particularly if you're up against healthcare professionals or educators who are reluctant to consider the possibility of autism. You might need to be persistent and assertive, especially if you're dealing with a system that is slow to recognize or respond to your concerns. Educating yourself about autism and the diagnostic process can help you feel more confident in advocating for your loved one. Don't be afraid to seek out second opinions or to push for further evaluation if you feel that your concerns are not being taken seriously.

Overcoming these barriers requires determination, resilience, and a willingness to advocate for yourself or your loved one. It's important to remember that seeking a diagnosis is not about fitting into a label—it's about understanding yourself or your loved one better and accessing the resources and support that can make life easier. By recognizing and addressing these barriers, you can move forward on your journey to diagnosis with greater confidence and clarity.

The Diagnostic Process: What to Expect

Once you've made the decision to pursue an autism diagnosis, it's helpful to know what to expect from the diagnostic process. This process can vary depending on your age, where you live, and the healthcare provider you see, but there are some common steps that most people will go through.

The first step in the diagnostic process is usually an initial consultation with a healthcare professional. This might be your primary care doctor, a psychologist, or a psychiatrist. During this consultation, you'll have the opportunity to discuss your concerns and why you believe you or your loved one might be autistic. The healthcare professional will likely ask you about your developmental history, including early childhood behaviors, social interactions, communication skills, and any challenges you've faced in school, work, or daily life. If you're seeking a diagnosis for a child, the doctor might ask you to fill out questionnaires or provide observations from teachers or other caregivers.

If the healthcare professional believes that further evaluation is warranted, they will likely refer you to a specialist who has experience in diagnosing autism. This specialist might be a clinical psychologist, a neuropsychologist, or a developmental pediatrician. The specialist will conduct a more in-depth assessment, which typically includes a combination of interviews, standardized tests, and behavioral observations.

One of the most common tools used in the diagnostic process is the Autism Diagnostic Observation Schedule (ADOS). The ADOS is a standardized assessment that involves a series of structured tasks and activities designed to elicit behaviors that are commonly associated with autism. The specialist will observe how you or your loved one responds to these tasks and will look for patterns of behavior that are characteristic of autism. This might include difficulties with social interaction, communication challenges, or repetitive behaviors.

In addition to the ADOS, the specialist might use other assessment tools, such as the Autism Diagnostic Interview-Revised (ADI-R), which is a detailed interview that explores developmental history and current behaviors. The specialist might also administer cognitive tests to assess areas like language, memory, and problem-solving skills. These tests can help differentiate autism from other conditions that might present with similar symptoms, such as ADHD or anxiety disorders.

Throughout the diagnostic process, the specialist will be looking for evidence of the core characteristics of autism: social communication difficulties, restricted interests, and repetitive behaviors. They will also consider how these characteristics have impacted your life or your loved one's life, both in the past and present. It's important to be as open and honest as possible during this process, even if it's difficult to talk about certain experiences. The more information the specialist has, the better they will be able to understand your unique profile and make an accurate diagnosis.

The diagnostic process can take several weeks or even months, depending on the availability of specialists and the complexity of the case. It's important to be patient and to take care of yourself during this time. The process can be emotionally taxing, especially if you're dealing with uncertainty or revisiting challenging experiences. Consider seeking support from friends, family, or a therapist who can help you navigate the emotional ups and downs of the diagnostic journey.

Once the assessment is complete, the specialist will provide you with a diagnosis. If you or your loved one is diagnosed with autism, the specialist will likely provide a detailed report that outlines the findings of the assessment and offers recommendations for support and intervention. This report can be an invaluable tool for accessing services, accommodations, and resources that can help you or your loved one thrive.

If the diagnosis is not autism, the specialist might suggest other possible explanations for the challenges you've been facing and provide recommendations for further evaluation or support. It's important to remember that the goal of the diagnostic process is not to label you or your loved one, but to provide a clearer understanding of your strengths and challenges so that you can access the support you need.

For some, receiving a diagnosis might come as a relief, providing clarity and validation for experiences that have been difficult to understand. For others, it might be more challenging to come to terms with the diagnosis, especially if it wasn't what you were expecting or if you have concerns about what it means for the future. It's important to give yourself or your loved one time to process the diagnosis and to seek out support if needed. Remember that a diagnosis is not the end of the journey—it's the beginning of a new chapter where you can start to access the resources and support that can help you or your loved one live a fulfilling life.

Coming to Terms with the Diagnosis

Receiving an autism diagnosis, whether for yourself or a loved one, can be a significant and emotional experience. It's natural to have a wide range of feelings in response to the diagnosis, and it's important to allow yourself the time and space to process these emotions. Coming to terms with the diagnosis is a personal journey, and there is no right or wrong way to feel.

For some, the diagnosis might bring a sense of relief and validation. You might finally have an explanation for the challenges you've faced and the feeling of being different that you've carried with you for much of your life. This newfound understanding can be empowering, allowing you to reframe your experiences and recognize your strengths as an autistic individual. It can also open the door to self-advocacy, where you can start to identify and communicate your needs, whether at work, in relationships, or in daily life.

However, it's also common to experience feelings of grief, loss, or even anger in response to an autism diagnosis. You might grieve the years spent struggling without understanding why, or you might feel a sense of loss for the life you imagined before the diagnosis. If the diagnosis is for a loved one, especially a child, you might worry about their future or feel uncertain about how to support them. These feelings are valid and normal, and it's important to acknowledge them rather than push them aside.

It's also worth noting that societal stigma and misconceptions about autism can contribute to feelings of shame or fear. You might worry about how others will perceive you or your loved one now that you have a diagnosis, or you might feel anxious about disclosing the diagnosis in certain settings. It's important to remember that autism is just one part of who you or your loved one is—it doesn't define you, and it doesn't change your worth or value as a person.

As you come to terms with the diagnosis, it can be helpful to seek out support from others who understand what you're going through. This might include joining support groups, either in person or online, where you can connect with others who have had similar experiences. Sharing your story and hearing from others can provide a sense of community and help you feel less alone in your journey. It can also be helpful to work with a therapist or counselor who has experience with autism, especially if you're struggling with feelings of anxiety, depression, or self-doubt.

Education is another important aspect of coming to terms with the diagnosis. Learning more about autism, including the strengths and challenges that come with it, can help you develop a more balanced and nuanced understanding of what it means to be autistic. This knowledge can also empower you to advocate for yourself or your loved one and to seek out the resources and support that can help you navigate the challenges you might face.

For parents or caregivers, coming to terms with a child's autism diagnosis might involve adjusting your expectations and finding new ways to support your child's development. It's important to focus on your child's strengths and to recognize that they have the potential to lead a fulfilling and meaningful life. Early intervention and support can make a significant difference, and there are many resources available to help you and your child navigate the challenges ahead.

It's also important to practice self-compassion as you come to terms with the diagnosis. Whether the diagnosis is for yourself or a loved one, it's natural to have moments of doubt or uncertainty. You might question whether you're doing enough, or you might worry about the future. It's important to be gentle with yourself and to recognize that this is a journey, not a destination. It's okay to have ups and downs, and it's okay to ask for help when you need it.

Ultimately, coming to terms with an autism diagnosis is about finding a sense of peace and acceptance. This doesn't mean that everything will be easy, but it does mean that you can approach the challenges ahead with a sense of understanding and self-compassion. Whether the diagnosis is for yourself or a loved one, remember that autism is just one part of who you are—it doesn't define you, and it doesn't limit your potential. With the right support and resources, you can navigate the journey ahead with confidence and resilience.

CHAPTER 3

SELF-IDENTITY AND ACCEPTANCE

Rediscovering Yourself After a Late Diagnosis

Receiving an autism diagnosis as an adult can feel like opening a door to a new world—one that's both familiar and foreign at the same time. On one hand, the diagnosis can validate the experiences and feelings that have shaped your life, offering an explanation for why certain things have always felt different. On the other hand, it can prompt a period of reflection and rediscovery as you begin to see yourself through this new lens. This process of rediscovering yourself is not just about understanding your autistic traits but also about reevaluating your past, present, and future with this new understanding in mind.

For many women, a late diagnosis can bring a profound sense of relief. You might finally have an answer to questions that have lingered for years—questions about why social interactions often felt like navigating a minefield, or why certain sensory experiences were overwhelming while others barely registered. This newfound clarity can help you reframe past experiences, recognizing that the challenges you faced were not due to personal failings but rather a different way of processing the world. This realization alone can be incredibly liberating, allowing you to forgive yourself for the times when you felt you didn't measure up to societal expectations.

However, along with the relief, you might also feel a sense of grief or loss. It's common to mourn the years spent struggling without knowing why or to feel sadness over the opportunities that might have been missed because you didn't have the right support or understanding. These feelings are natural and valid, and it's important to give yourself the time and space to process them. Rediscovering yourself after a late diagnosis is not just about moving forward; it's also about coming to terms with the past.

As you begin this journey of rediscovery, it can be helpful to revisit key moments in your life with your new understanding in mind. Reflect on your childhood, your teenage years, and your experiences as an adult. How did your autistic traits shape these experiences? Were there times when you felt particularly misunderstood or isolated? Were there moments of triumph that you now recognize as a testament to your resilience as an autistic woman? This process of reflection can help you make sense of your life story, allowing you to weave together the threads of your identity in a way that feels more coherent and true to who you are.

This process of rediscovery is also about reclaiming your identity. For many women, the pressure to conform to societal norms can lead to a lifetime of masking—hiding or suppressing autistic traits in order to fit in. This might have meant forcing yourself to engage in social activities that drained you, enduring sensory experiences that were overwhelming, or pretending to understand conversations that felt like they were in a foreign language. Over time, this masking can take a toll, leading to feelings of burnout, anxiety, and a sense of being disconnected from your true self.

Now that you have a diagnosis, you have the opportunity to let go of the mask and embrace your authentic self. This might feel daunting at first, especially if you've spent years perfecting the art of masking. But it can also be incredibly freeing to acknowledge your needs, set boundaries, and express yourself in ways that feel natural to you. This might mean saying no to social events that you find overwhelming, seeking out quiet spaces when you need to recharge, or indulging in your special interests without feeling the need to hide them. Rediscovering yourself after a late diagnosis is about giving yourself permission to be who you are, without apology or explanation.

As you go through this journey, it's important to remember that there is no right or wrong way to be autistic. Your experiences, preferences, and traits are all valid, and they are all part of what makes you uniquely you. Embracing your autistic identity doesn't mean that you have to fit a particular mold or adhere to certain stereotypes. It's about understanding yourself on your own terms and finding ways to live that honor your true self.

Self-Acceptance and Embracing Neurodiversity

Self-acceptance is a key part of the journey toward embracing your identity as an autistic woman. It involves acknowledging your strengths and challenges, understanding your unique way of experiencing the world, and being kind to yourself in the face of societal pressures to conform. For many women, this journey toward self-acceptance is intertwined with the broader concept of neurodiversity—the idea that there is a natural variation in how human brains are wired, and that these differences should be celebrated rather than pathologized.

Embracing neurodiversity means recognizing that your brain works differently, and that's okay. It's not something that needs to be fixed or cured. Instead, it's something that can bring richness and diversity to the human experience. By embracing your neurodivergence, you're also challenging the societal norms that have long dictated what is considered "normal" or "acceptable." This can be a powerful and empowering shift in perspective, one that allows you to take pride in your identity rather than feeling pressured to conform.

Self-acceptance also involves letting go of the internalized ableism that many autistic women have absorbed over the years. This might include beliefs that you need to change who you are to be accepted, that your differences are flaws, or that you should be able to do things the same way as neurotypical people. These beliefs are often reinforced by societal messages that prioritize conformity and sameness, but they are not truths. Challenging these beliefs can be difficult, especially if they've been ingrained for a long time, but it's an essential part of embracing your identity.

One way to start building self-acceptance is to focus on your strengths and what you bring to the world as an autistic woman. Maybe you have a keen attention to detail, a deep well of knowledge about your special interests, or a unique way of seeing problems that allows you to find creative solutions. These are all strengths that deserve to be celebrated. By shifting your focus from what you struggle with to what you excel at, you can start to build a more balanced and positive self-image.

It's also important to surround yourself with people who support and accept you as you are. This might mean seeking out communities of other autistic women or neurodivergent individuals who understand and share your experiences. Being part of a community that values neurodiversity can be incredibly validating and can help reinforce your journey toward self-acceptance. These communities can also provide a space to share strategies for navigating challenges, celebrate successes, and connect with others who "get it."

Another key aspect of embracing neurodiversity is advocating for yourself and others. This might involve speaking up about your needs in the workplace, educating others about autism, or challenging misconceptions when you encounter them. Advocacy can be a powerful tool for building self-acceptance because it shifts the focus from trying to fit into a neurotypical world to creating a world that recognizes and accommodates neurodiversity. By advocating for your rights and the rights of others, you're also affirming your worth and the value of neurodivergent perspectives.

Self-acceptance is a journey, and it's one that might take time. There will likely be moments of doubt, frustration, or self-criticism along the way, and that's okay. What's important is to keep moving forward, to keep challenging the negative beliefs that hold you back, and to keep embracing the idea that you are enough, just as you are. Remember that self-acceptance doesn't mean that you have to love every aspect of yourself all the time—it means recognizing your worth and treating yourself with the same kindness and compassion that you would offer to a friend.

Building Self-Esteem and Confidence

Building self-esteem and confidence as an autistic woman is an important part of the journey toward self-acceptance. Self-esteem is about how you perceive your own worth, while confidence is about believing in your ability to handle challenges and succeed in various areas of life. For many autistic women, these qualities can be difficult to cultivate, especially if you've faced a lifetime of misunderstanding, marginalization, or feeling like you don't quite fit in. However, building self-esteem and confidence is possible, and it's a crucial part of living a fulfilling and empowered life.

One of the first steps in building self-esteem is to challenge the negative self-perceptions that might have taken root over the years. These perceptions often stem from societal messages that prioritize neurotypical ways of being and devalue neurodivergent experiences. You might have internalized beliefs that you're not good enough, that your differences are shortcomings, or that you'll never measure up to the standards set by others. These beliefs are not truths—they are reflections of a society that doesn't fully understand or appreciate neurodiversity. Challenging these beliefs involves recognizing where they come from, questioning their validity, and replacing them with more empowering and supportive thoughts.

Another important aspect of building self-esteem is to recognize and celebrate your achievements, no matter how big or small they may seem. It's easy to focus on what you haven't accomplished or where you've fallen short, but this perspective doesn't do justice to the many things you've done well. Take the time to acknowledge your successes, whether it's mastering a new skill, navigating a difficult social situation, or simply taking care of yourself during a challenging time. Celebrating these achievements can help reinforce a positive self-image and remind you of your capabilities.

Confidence, like self-esteem, is built through experience and practice. One way to build confidence is to set small, achievable goals for yourself and work toward them step by step. These goals don't have to be grand or life-changing—they can be as simple as trying a new activity, speaking up in a meeting, or taking on a new responsibility at work. Each time you achieve one of these goals, you're proving to yourself that you can handle challenges and succeed. Over time, these small successes can build up, creating a strong foundation of confidence that you can draw on in other areas of your life. As you achieve these goals, take note of the progress you've made and use it as a reminder of your ability to tackle challenges and grow. Building confidence is about gradually expanding your comfort zone and recognizing that you have the skills and resilience to overcome obstacles.

Another effective strategy for building confidence is to surround yourself with supportive and encouraging people. Having a strong support network can make a significant difference in how you view yourself and your abilities. Seek out mentors, friends, or colleagues who recognize your strengths and offer positive reinforcement. Their encouragement can help counteract self-doubt and reinforce your belief in your own capabilities.

It's also valuable to engage in activities that align with your interests and passions. When you do things that you love and excel at, it can boost your self-esteem and confidence. Whether it's pursuing a hobby, engaging in creative projects, or excelling in your professional field, immersing yourself in activities that bring you joy and satisfaction can help reinforce a positive self-image.

Remember that building self-esteem and confidence is a continuous process. It requires ongoing effort and self-reflection. There may be setbacks along the way, and that's okay. What's important is to stay committed to nurturing a positive self-view and to practice self-compassion when you encounter challenges. Be patient with yourself and recognize that progress may come gradually.

Additionally, developing a growth mindset can be beneficial. A growth mindset is the belief that abilities and intelligence can be developed through effort, learning, and perseverance. Adopting this mindset can help you approach challenges with a sense of curiosity and determination rather than fear of failure. It encourages you to see setbacks as opportunities for growth rather than reflections of your worth. By cultivating a growth mindset, you can build resilience and confidence in your ability to learn and adapt.

Navigating the Emotional Journey

Navigating the emotional journey of self-acceptance and identity as an autistic woman involves recognizing and addressing a wide range of feelings. This journey can be filled with moments of self-discovery, empowerment, and also challenges and uncertainties. It's important to approach this emotional landscape with sensitivity and self-compassion, acknowledging that each person's experience is unique and valid.

One common emotional experience is a sense of grief or loss, especially if you've spent years struggling without understanding why. You might mourn missed opportunities or the challenges you faced due to a lack of support. It's important to allow yourself to feel these emotions without judgment. Grieving is a natural part of processing the impact of a late diagnosis and coming to terms with your past experiences. Speaking with a therapist or counselor who specializes in autism can be helpful in navigating these feelings and finding ways to move forward.

At the same time, the emotional journey can also be marked by moments of joy and empowerment. Understanding your autism can lead to a profound sense of validation and self-awareness. You might feel a renewed sense of purpose or excitement about embracing your neurodivergent identity. These positive emotions are equally important and can serve as a source of motivation and strength as you continue on your journey.

One of the challenges you might face is managing societal expectations and pressures. Society often has specific norms and standards that can make it difficult for neurodivergent individuals to feel accepted or understood. You might encounter misunderstandings or face pressure to conform to neurotypical standards. It's important to recognize that these external pressures do not define your worth or value. Navigating societal expectations involves finding a balance between honoring your authentic self and engaging with the world in a way that feels manageable and authentic to you.

Building emotional resilience is another key aspect of navigating this journey. Resilience involves developing coping strategies and finding ways to manage stress and setbacks. It can be helpful to identify strategies that work for you, such as mindfulness practices, self-care routines, or engaging in activities that bring you joy. Resilience is about acknowledging your feelings, finding healthy ways to cope with challenges, and continuing to move forward even when faced with difficulties.

Throughout this journey, it's also important to practice self-compassion. Be kind to yourself as you steer through the complexities of self-identity and acceptance. Recognize that it's okay to have moments of doubt or uncertainty and that these feelings are a natural part of the process. Treat yourself with the same empathy and understanding that you would offer to a friend who is going through a similar experience.

Finally, connecting with others who share similar experiences can provide valuable support and validation. Whether through support groups, online communities, or in-person gatherings, finding a sense of belonging with others who understand your journey can be incredibly affirming. These connections can offer insights, encouragement, and a sense of solidarity as you navigate your emotional journey.

CHAPTER 4

MANAGING DAILY LIFE

Executive Functioning Challenges and Solutions

Going through daily life with executive functioning challenges can feel like trying to complete a complex puzzle where the pieces don't always fit together smoothly. Executive functioning refers to a set of cognitive processes that help us plan, organize, and execute tasks. These skills are crucial for managing daily responsibilities, but they can be particularly challenging for many autistic women. Understanding these challenges and finding practical solutions can make a significant difference in managing your daily life more effectively.

One common executive functioning challenge is difficulty with planning and organizing tasks. You might find it hard to break down large projects into manageable steps or struggle to keep track of multiple tasks and deadlines. This can lead to feelings of overwhelm and frustration, especially when trying to juggle various responsibilities. To address this challenge, try using visual aids such as planners, calendars, or task management apps. Breaking tasks into smaller, more manageable steps and setting specific deadlines for each step can help make large projects feel less daunting.

Creating a structured routine can also be beneficial. Routines provide a sense of predictability and can help reduce the cognitive load associated with planning and decision-making. Establishing daily or weekly routines for specific tasks, such as meal planning, cleaning, or work-related activities, can help streamline your activities and reduce the mental effort required to manage them. Consistent routines can also provide a comforting structure, making it easier to navigate your day.

Another challenge with executive functioning is managing distractions and maintaining focus. Many autistic individuals find it difficult to concentrate on tasks, especially in environments with multiple stimuli. To improve focus, consider creating a dedicated workspace that minimizes distractions. This might involve using noise-canceling headphones, setting up a quiet corner, or employing tools like website blockers to limit online distractions. Additionally, incorporating regular breaks into your work or study sessions can help maintain focus and prevent burnout.

Time management is another area where executive functioning challenges often arise. You might struggle with estimating how long tasks will take, leading to issues with deadlines or procrastination. To improve time management, try using timers or alarms to track time spent on tasks. Setting specific time limits for each activity and using visual reminders can help keep you on track. Additionally, practice prioritizing tasks based on urgency and importance, and be realistic about what you can achieve within a given timeframe.

Developing strategies for managing executive functioning challenges often involves trial and error. What works for one person might not work for another, so it's important to experiment with different approaches and find what suits your individual needs. Seeking support from professionals such as occupational therapists or coaches who specialize in executive functioning can also provide valuable guidance and tailored strategies.

Time Management and Organization Strategies

Effective time management and organization are crucial skills for managing daily life, and they can be particularly challenging for autistic women. Finding strategies that work for you can help streamline your daily activities, reduce stress, and increase your overall productivity. Let's explore some practical strategies to enhance your time management and organizational skills.

One effective strategy for managing time is creating a detailed schedule or planner. This can help you visualize your daily, weekly, or monthly tasks and deadlines. Whether you use a physical planner or a digital calendar, having a clear overview of your responsibilities can help you stay organized and on track. Be sure to include not only work or school-related tasks but also personal commitments and self-care activities.

Breaking tasks into smaller, more manageable chunks can also improve your time management. Instead of tackling a large project all at once, divide it into smaller tasks with specific deadlines. This approach makes the project feel less overwhelming and helps you maintain focus. For example, if you're working on a report, break it down into steps like research, outlining, drafting, and revising. Assign deadlines to each step to keep yourself on track.

To stay organized, consider using tools like to-do lists or task management apps. These tools can help you keep track of tasks, set priorities, and monitor your progress. Create daily or weekly to-do lists and prioritize tasks based on their urgency and importance. Checking off completed tasks can provide a sense of accomplishment and help you stay motivated.

Time management also involves setting boundaries and managing your time effectively. Learn to say no to additional commitments if you're already feeling overwhelmed. Setting boundaries helps prevent burnout and ensures that you have enough time for self-care and relaxation. It's important to recognize your limits and avoid overloading yourself with too many tasks.

Another useful technique for improving time management is the Pomodoro Technique. This method involves working in short, focused intervals (usually 25 minutes) followed by a brief break. After completing a few intervals, take a longer break. This technique can help maintain focus and prevent fatigue. Adjust the intervals and breaks to fit your needs and preferences.

Creating a dedicated workspace can also enhance your organizational skills. A clutter-free and well-organized workspace can reduce distractions and help you stay focused. Keep essential items within reach and use organizational tools like folders, trays, or bins to keep your workspace tidy. Establishing a designated area for work or study can help signal to your brain that it's time to focus.

Time management and organization are ongoing skills that can be refined and improved over time. Experiment with different strategies, and be open to adjusting your approach as needed. Regularly review and update your systems to ensure they continue to meet your needs and help you stay on top of your responsibilities.

Coping with Sensory Overload

Sensory overload can be a significant challenge for many autistic women. It occurs when the sensory input from the environment becomes overwhelming and difficult to process. This can lead to feelings of stress, anxiety, or even physical discomfort. Understanding how to cope with sensory overload can help you manage these experiences and improve your overall well-being.

One effective strategy for coping with sensory overload is to create a sensory-friendly environment. Identify the specific sensory inputs that contribute to your overload, such as bright lights, loud noises, or strong smells. Once you've identified these triggers, take steps to minimize or eliminate them in your environment. For example, using dim lighting, noise-canceling headphones, or scented candles can help create a more comfortable space.

Having a sensory toolkit can also be helpful. This toolkit might include items or activities that help you calm down and regulate your sensory input. For example, fidget toys, weighted blankets, or soothing music can provide sensory input that helps you feel more grounded. Carrying a small bag with these items can provide a sense of security and offer a quick way to manage sensory overload when it arises.

Developing coping strategies for managing sensory overload can also involve practicing mindfulness or relaxation techniques. Mindfulness involves paying attention to the present moment without judgment, which can help you stay grounded and reduce stress. Techniques such as deep breathing, progressive muscle relaxation, or guided imagery can help calm your nervous system and alleviate feelings of overwhelm.

Creating a personal sensory routine can also be beneficial. This routine might include regular activities or breaks that help you manage sensory input throughout the day. For example, scheduling quiet breaks or engaging in calming activities like reading or taking a walk can help you recharge and reduce the impact of sensory overload.

It's also important to communicate your sensory needs to others when appropriate. Letting friends, family, or colleagues know about your sensory sensitivities can help them understand and accommodate your needs. Open communication can lead to more supportive interactions and a greater understanding of how to create a comfortable environment for you.

If sensory overload becomes a frequent or severe issue, seeking support from a therapist or occupational therapist who specializes in sensory processing can be helpful. These professionals can work with you to develop tailored strategies and interventions that address your specific sensory needs.

Navigating Social Interactions

Social interactions can be complex and challenging for many autistic women. Understanding and navigating social norms, cues, and expectations can sometimes feel like trying to decode an elaborate and ever-changing code. However, with the right strategies and support, you can develop skills and confidence to handle social interactions more effectively.

One key aspect of navigating social interactions is understanding and interpreting social cues. This includes nonverbal cues such as body language, facial expressions, and tone of voice. While these cues can be subtle and complex, practicing observation and paying attention to these details can help you improve your understanding of social dynamics. You might also find it helpful to ask for feedback from trusted friends or mentors who can provide insights into how you're interpreting social cues.

Another important strategy is to develop and practice social scripts. Social scripts are pre-planned responses or strategies for common social situations. For example, you might prepare a few conversation starters or responses for social gatherings. Having these scripts in mind can help reduce anxiety and provide a sense of preparedness when engaging in social interactions.

Setting boundaries is another crucial aspect of navigating social interactions. It's important to recognize and communicate your boundaries to others, whether it's about personal space, communication preferences, or sensory sensitivities. Setting clear and respectful boundaries can help create a more comfortable and respectful social environment for you.

Developing self-advocacy skills is also important. Self-advocacy involves expressing your needs, preferences, and limitations in a clear and assertive manner. This might include communicating your sensory needs, discussing accommodations, or expressing your feelings about social interactions. Practicing self-advocacy can empower you to navigate social situations more effectively and ensure that your needs are understood and respected.

Building social skills takes practice and patience. Engaging in social activities, joining interest-based groups, or participating in community events can provide opportunities to practice and refine your social skills. Start with smaller or more manageable social interactions and gradually work your way up to larger or more complex situations. Remember that it's okay to take breaks or step back if you need to recharge.

Finally, be kind to yourself as you navigate social interactions. It's natural to make mistakes or feel unsure at times. Recognize that social interactions are a learning process and that you're continuously growing and improving. Celebrate your successes, no matter how small, and remember that each experience contributes to your overall growth and understanding.

CHAPTER 5

RELATIONSHIPS AND SOCIAL CONNECTIONS

Family Dynamics and Autism

Family dynamics can be both a source of support and a challenge for autistic women. Understanding how autism impacts family relationships and finding ways to navigate these dynamics can improve family interactions and create a more supportive environment.

Autistic individuals often experience family dynamics differently due to variations in communication styles, sensory sensitivities, and social expectations. For instance, a family member might struggle with sensory overload during family gatherings, while others might have difficulty understanding these sensory needs. This disconnect can lead to misunderstandings or unintentional conflict. It's essential to communicate openly about your needs and preferences, helping family members understand how they can support you better. Sharing information about autism and its impact on your daily life can also bridge gaps in understanding and foster empathy within the family.

Family members may also have their own experiences and perspectives regarding autism, which can influence family dynamics. For example, siblings might feel overlooked or misunderstood if the focus is primarily on the autistic family member. Encouraging open dialogue and providing opportunities for all family members to express their feelings can help address these issues. Family therapy or counseling can also be beneficial in navigating complex family dynamics and improving communication.

Navigating family gatherings and holidays can be particularly challenging. To manage these events more comfortably, consider discussing potential adjustments or accommodations in advance. This might include arranging for quiet spaces, modifying the schedule, or preparing sensory-friendly environments. Setting realistic expectations for yourself and your family can help reduce stress and create a more enjoyable experience.

It's also important to recognize and celebrate the strengths and contributions of autistic family members. Autism often brings unique perspectives and skills that can enrich family life. By acknowledging and valuing these strengths, you can help create a more inclusive and supportive family environment.

Building and Maintaining Friendships

Building and maintaining friendships can be a rewarding but sometimes challenging experience for autistic women. Developing meaningful connections involves understanding social cues, navigating communication styles, and finding common interests.

Starting and sustaining friendships often begins with finding shared interests or activities. Engaging in hobbies, joining clubs, or participating in community events related to your interests can provide opportunities to meet like-minded individuals. Shared interests can serve as a foundation for conversations and help build rapport with others.

When it comes to initiating and maintaining friendships, clear communication is key. Autistic individuals may have different communication styles, which can sometimes lead to misunderstandings. Being open and honest about your communication preferences can help set the stage for clearer interactions. For example, you might prefer direct and straightforward conversations rather than ambiguous or indirect communication. Sharing your preferences with potential friends can foster mutual understanding and improve the quality of interactions.

Friendships require effort and reciprocity. Maintaining a friendship involves regular communication, showing interest in the other person's life, and being supportive. Scheduling regular catch-ups, whether through phone calls, texts, or in-person meetings, helps keep the connection strong. Additionally, showing empathy and understanding towards your friend's experiences and challenges can strengthen the bond between you.

Building and maintaining friendships also involves setting boundaries. It's important to recognize your limits and communicate them clearly to your friends. For example, if you need time alone to recharge or have specific sensory sensitivities, sharing these needs with your friends can help them understand and respect your boundaries. Setting and respecting boundaries contributes to healthier and more sustainable friendships.

Navigating social interactions and building friendships can sometimes be overwhelming. Seeking support from social skills groups, online communities, or therapy can provide valuable guidance and practice. These resources can offer strategies for improving social skills and building confidence in social situations.

Romantic Relationships: Understanding and Communication

Romantic relationships bring unique challenges and opportunities for autistic women. Understanding how autism influences romantic relationships and developing effective communication strategies can enhance the quality of your relationships and foster deeper connections.

Effective communication is a cornerstone of successful romantic relationships. Autistic individuals may have different communication styles and preferences, which can impact how you express yourself and understand your partner. Open and honest communication about your needs, expectations, and any challenges you face is crucial for building a strong foundation. Discussing topics such as sensory sensitivities, social preferences, and emotional needs can help your partner understand and support you better.

Romantic relationships often involve navigating emotional expression and understanding. Autistic individuals might experience and express emotions differently, which can sometimes lead to misunderstandings with partners. Exploring and discussing your emotional experiences and how you express them can help your partner gain insight into your emotional world. Additionally, learning about and practicing different ways to express affection and emotional support can strengthen your connection.

Boundaries and personal space are also important considerations in romantic relationships. Autistic individuals may have specific needs regarding physical space or sensory input, and it's essential to communicate these needs to your partner. Setting clear boundaries and discussing your preferences can help create a respectful and comfortable environment for both partners.

Building and maintaining a romantic relationship also involves mutual respect and understanding. It's important for both partners to recognize and appreciate each other's strengths and differences. Embracing each other's unique qualities and working together to address any challenges can strengthen the relationship and foster a deeper connection.

If navigating romantic relationships becomes challenging, seeking support from a therapist or counselor who specializes in relationships and autism can be beneficial. Professional guidance can provide strategies for improving communication, managing relationship dynamics, and addressing any issues that arise.

Parenting as an Autistic Woman

Parenting presents its own set of challenges and rewards, and being an autistic woman adds a unique perspective to the parenting experience. Understanding how autism influences parenting and finding effective strategies can help you navigate the journey of parenthood successfully.

One key aspect of parenting as an autistic woman is understanding your own needs and limitations. Recognizing how autism impacts your sensory sensitivities, communication styles, and executive functioning can help you develop strategies to manage parenting responsibilities. For example, establishing a structured routine and creating a sensory-friendly environment can benefit both you and your child.

Building a support network is also crucial for parenting. Connecting with other autistic parents, joining parenting support groups, or seeking guidance from professionals can provide valuable insights and support. Sharing experiences and strategies with others who understand your perspective can be empowering and reassuring.

Effective communication with your child is essential. Autistic individuals may have different communication styles, and finding ways to adapt your communication to meet your child's needs can enhance your relationship. Using visual aids, clear language, and consistent routines can help facilitate communication and understanding.

Self-care is another important aspect of parenting. Balancing the demands of parenting with your own needs and well-being is crucial. Prioritizing self-care, setting realistic expectations, and seeking support when needed can help you manage the challenges of parenting while maintaining your own health and happiness.

Parenting as an autistic woman can also offer unique strengths and perspectives. Embracing your strengths, such as attention to detail, creativity, or problem-solving skills, can enrich your parenting experience. Recognizing and valuing these strengths can contribute to a positive and fulfilling parenting journey.

CHAPTER 6

MENTAL HEALTH AND WELL-BEING

Common Co-Occurring Conditions

Autistic adult women often experience co-occurring mental health conditions, which can impact their overall well-being. Among these, anxiety and depression are particularly common, though there are others that may also affect you. Understanding these conditions, their symptoms, and how they intersect with autism can provide valuable insights into managing your mental health.

Anxiety disorders are prevalent among autistic individuals. Symptoms of anxiety might include excessive worry, panic attacks, or a constant feeling of apprehension. For autistic women, anxiety can be triggered by sensory overload, social interactions, or changes in routine. The heightened sensitivity to sensory inputs and the stress of navigating social expectations can exacerbate feelings of anxiety. Strategies to manage anxiety often involve recognizing and addressing these triggers. Techniques such as deep breathing, cognitive-behavioral strategies, and structured routines can help mitigate anxiety symptoms.

Depression is another common co-occurring condition. Symptoms may include persistent sadness, loss of interest in activities, fatigue, and feelings of worthlessness. For autistic women, depression may be influenced by factors such as social isolation, difficulty in communication, or sensory overload. Recognizing the signs of depression and seeking appropriate support is crucial.

Early intervention and addressing the underlying factors contributing to depression can improve your quality of life.

Other co-occurring conditions include obsessive-compulsive disorder (OCD), which involves repetitive thoughts and behaviors, and attention-deficit/hyperactivity disorder (ADHD), which affects attention and impulse control. Each condition interacts uniquely with autism, and managing these conditions requires a tailored approach. For instance, if you experience OCD, incorporating structured routines and cognitive-behavioral techniques can be beneficial. Understanding how these co-occurring conditions impact you and seeking appropriate treatment can lead to better overall mental health.

Strategies for Managing Stress and Burnout

Stress and burnout are significant concerns for autistic adult women, often arising from the demands of daily life, social interactions, and sensory overload. Implementing effective strategies to manage stress and prevent burnout is essential for maintaining your well-being.

One effective strategy for managing stress is creating a structured routine. Establishing a predictable daily schedule can help reduce uncertainty and provide a sense of control. This structure allows you to plan your activities, manage your time effectively, and incorporate breaks into your day. By creating a routine that works for you, you can minimize stressors and enhance your overall stability.

Another approach is practicing time management and setting realistic goals.

Breaking tasks into smaller, manageable steps and prioritizing them can prevent feelings of overwhelm. Use tools such as planners, to-do lists, or time management apps to keep track of your responsibilities and deadlines. Setting achievable goals and celebrating your progress can also contribute to reducing stress and avoiding burnout.

Incorporating relaxation techniques into your daily routine can help manage stress. Techniques such as deep breathing exercises, progressive muscle relaxation, and guided imagery can promote relaxation and reduce the physiological symptoms of stress. Finding what works best for you and making time for these practices regularly can improve your ability to handle stress.

It's also important to recognize and address signs of burnout early. Burnout often manifests as physical and emotional exhaustion, reduced performance, and a sense of detachment. Pay attention to signs such as persistent fatigue, irritability, or a lack of motivation. When you notice these signs, take proactive steps to address them, such as adjusting your workload, taking breaks, or seeking support.

Self-care is a crucial component of managing stress and preventing burnout. Prioritize activities that promote your well-being, such as engaging in hobbies, spending time in nature, or practicing mindfulness. Making time for self-care and setting boundaries to protect your personal time can help you recharge and maintain balance.

Mindfulness and Self-Care Practices

Mindfulness and self-care practices play a significant role in maintaining mental health and well-being for autistic adult women. These practices can help manage stress, enhance emotional regulation, and improve overall quality of life.

Mindfulness involves paying attention to the present moment with acceptance and without judgment. It can help you become more aware of your thoughts, feelings, and bodily sensations, leading to a greater understanding of yourself. Mindfulness techniques, such as mindful breathing, body scans, and mindful eating, can help you stay grounded and manage stress. Regular practice of mindfulness can enhance your ability to respond to stressors in a calm and measured way.

Incorporating self-care practices into your routine is equally important. Self-care encompasses activities that promote physical, emotional, and mental well-being. This might include engaging in hobbies, practicing relaxation techniques, or maintaining a healthy lifestyle through exercise and balanced nutrition. Identifying activities that bring you joy and relaxation and making time for them regularly can contribute to a sense of fulfillment and well-being.

Creating a self-care routine that fits your needs and preferences can enhance its effectiveness. For instance, if you find that physical activity helps you manage stress, incorporate regular exercise into your routine. If you enjoy creative activities, such as painting or writing, set aside time for these activities as a form of relaxation. Tailoring your self-care routine to your individual needs can lead to more effective and enjoyable practices.

Developing a mindfulness practice can also involve integrating mindfulness into daily activities. Practicing mindfulness while engaging in routine tasks, such as washing dishes or walking, can help you stay present and reduce stress. Over time, these practices can become a natural part of your daily life, contributing to overall well-being.

Seeking Professional Support

Seeking professional support is an important step in managing mental health and well-being, particularly when dealing with co-occurring conditions, stress, or burnout. Professional support can provide valuable guidance, tools, and strategies to address mental health challenges effectively.

Therapy and counseling are common forms of professional support. Cognitive-behavioral therapy (CBT) is often used to address issues such as anxiety and depression. CBT focuses on identifying and changing negative thought patterns and behaviors. Other therapeutic approaches, such as acceptance and commitment therapy (ACT) or dialectical behavior therapy (DBT), may also be beneficial, depending on your specific needs.

Finding a therapist or counselor who has experience working with autistic individuals can be particularly valuable. An experienced professional will have a better understanding of how autism intersects with mental health and can provide tailored support. Look for therapists who specialize in autism or who have experience working with neurodiverse individuals.

In addition to individual therapy, support groups can provide a sense of community and connection. Joining a support group for autistic women can offer opportunities to share experiences, gain insights, and receive support from others who understand your perspective. Support groups can also provide practical advice and strategies for managing mental health and well-being.

Medication may also be a component of managing mental health conditions. If you experience symptoms of anxiety, depression, or other co-occurring conditions, consult with a healthcare provider to explore treatment options. Medication can be an effective tool in conjunction with therapy and self-care practices.

Overall, seeking professional support involves identifying your needs and finding appropriate resources. Whether through therapy, support groups, or medication, professional support can provide valuable assistance in managing mental health and improving your overall well-being.

CHAPTER 7

EMPLOYMENT AND CAREER DEVELOPMENT

Finding the Right Career Path

Finding the right career path can be a particularly nuanced journey for autistic adult women. The process involves exploring your interests, strengths, and values, and aligning them with a career that suits your unique needs and preferences. It starts with self-discovery: understanding what you enjoy, what you're good at, and what kind of work environment supports you best.

One of the first steps is to reflect on your passions and strengths. What activities or tasks do you find most engaging? What are you naturally good at? Identifying these areas can help you narrow down potential career options. For example, if you have a strong affinity for detail-oriented tasks and enjoy working with data, careers in research or data analysis might be a good fit. Conversely, if you have a passion for creativity and visual design, careers in graphic design or art might be more fulfilling.

Next, consider the work environment that best suits your sensory and social preferences. Some autistic individuals thrive in highly structured environments with clear expectations and minimal sensory distractions, while others may prefer more flexible and creative settings. Reflect on what type of work environment aligns with your sensory needs and communication style. For instance, a quieter, more controlled workspace might be ideal if you are sensitive to noise, while a collaborative and dynamic environment could be better if you enjoy teamwork and social interaction.

It can also be helpful to explore various career options through internships, volunteer work, or part-time positions. Gaining firsthand experience in different fields can provide valuable insights into what you enjoy and what suits you best. Additionally, talking to professionals in your areas of interest can offer practical advice and help you understand the day-to-day realities of different careers.

Career assessments and counseling can be useful tools in this process. Professional career counselors can provide guidance and support tailored to your individual needs. They can help you explore your interests and strengths and identify career paths that align with your goals. Additionally, online career assessments and tools can offer insights into potential career options based on your preferences and skills.

Navigating the Workplace: Rights and Accommodations

Navigating the workplace effectively involves understanding your rights and advocating for necessary accommodations. Autistic individuals may require specific adjustments to thrive in a work environment, and knowing how to request and negotiate these accommodations can make a significant difference in your career success.

Under various laws and regulations, including the Americans with Disabilities Act (ADA) in the United States, individuals with disabilities, including autism, are entitled to reasonable accommodations in the workplace. These accommodations are intended to provide you with equal opportunities to perform your job effectively. Common accommodations might include modifications to your work environment, such as noise-canceling headphones, flexible work hours, or changes to communication methods.

To request accommodations, start by identifying the specific challenges you face in the workplace and how they impact your performance. Clearly communicate your needs to your employer, providing detailed information about the accommodations that would support your success. It's often helpful to provide examples of how these accommodations will enable you to perform your job effectively.

Open and transparent communication with your employer is crucial. Approach the conversation with a focus on how the requested accommodations will enhance your productivity and contribute to the overall success of the team. Emphasize that the accommodations are intended to help you perform at your best, rather than as a form of preferential treatment.

It's also important to be aware of your rights and protections as an employee. Familiarize yourself with relevant employment laws and regulations, and seek guidance from legal or advocacy organizations if needed. Understanding your rights can empower you to advocate for yourself and ensure that you receive the support you are entitled to.

Building a positive and proactive relationship with your employer can also facilitate a smoother accommodation process. Maintain open lines of communication, provide regular updates on your needs, and be flexible in working with your employer to find effective solutions. By collaborating with your employer and demonstrating your commitment to your role, you can foster a supportive and inclusive work environment.

Communication Skills for Professional Success

Effective communication is a key component of professional success, and developing strong communication skills can significantly enhance your career prospects. For autistic adult women, this involves understanding and adapting to various communication styles and expectations in the workplace.

One essential aspect of communication in a professional setting is clarity. Clearly articulating your ideas, thoughts, and needs helps ensure that your message is understood and minimizes the risk of misunderstandings. Practice expressing yourself in a concise and straightforward manner, and consider using written communication, such as emails or reports, to complement verbal interactions when necessary.

Active listening is another crucial communication skill. This involves not only hearing what others are saying but also understanding and responding appropriately. Active listening includes maintaining eye contact, nodding, and providing feedback or clarifications as needed. Engaging in active listening helps build rapport with colleagues and demonstrates your attentiveness and respect for their perspectives.

Adaptability in communication is also important. Different situations and individuals may require varying communication styles. For example, some colleagues may prefer direct and detailed communication, while others may appreciate a more casual approach. Observing and adapting to these preferences can improve your interactions and enhance your effectiveness in the workplace.

Non-verbal communication, such as body language and facial expressions, plays a significant role in professional interactions. Being aware of your own non-verbal cues and interpreting those of others can help you navigate social dynamics and convey your messages more effectively. If non-verbal communication is challenging, consider discussing strategies with a therapist or counselor who specializes in social skills.

Building and maintaining professional relationships involves networking and relationship-building skills. Attend industry events, engage in professional organizations, and connect with colleagues and mentors to expand your network. Developing strong professional relationships can provide valuable support, guidance, and opportunities for career advancement.

Thriving in a Neurotypical Work Environment

Thriving in a neurotypical work environment involves finding ways to adapt to and excel in settings that may have different social and sensory expectations than what you are accustomed to. It's about leveraging your strengths while addressing challenges to create a successful and fulfilling career.

One approach to thriving in a neurotypical work environment is to identify and utilize your unique strengths. Autistic individuals often possess valuable skills, such as attention to detail, analytical thinking, and creativity. Highlight these strengths in your work and seek opportunities that allow you to leverage them. By focusing on your strengths, you can contribute significantly to your team and excel in your role.

Developing strategies to manage sensory sensitivities and social interactions is also crucial. For instance, if you find certain sensory inputs overwhelming, consider using noise-canceling headphones or taking breaks in a quiet space. Establishing boundaries and setting up a sensory-friendly workspace can help you manage sensory overload and maintain focus.

Social interactions in a neurotypical work environment may require additional effort. Navigating office politics, participating in social events, and understanding unspoken social norms can be challenging. To address this, observe and learn from colleagues, and seek feedback or mentorship from trusted individuals. Developing social skills and building rapport with colleagues can enhance your workplace experience and foster a positive work environment.

Time management and organization are essential for thriving in a neurotypical work environment. Implement strategies such as using planners, setting reminders, and breaking tasks into smaller steps to stay organized and meet deadlines. Creating a structured routine and prioritizing tasks can help you manage your workload effectively and reduce stress.

Finally, remember that thriving in a neurotypical work environment is an ongoing process of adaptation and self-care. Regularly assess your needs, seek feedback, and make adjustments as necessary. Embrace your unique qualities, celebrate your successes, and continue to seek opportunities for growth and development in your career.

CHAPTER 9

FINANCIAL INDEPENDENCE AND PLANNING

Managing Finances as an Autistic Adult

Achieving financial independence is a significant milestone for many autistic adults, and managing your finances effectively is a crucial part of this journey. For autistic adult women, financial management may involve unique challenges, such as navigating complex financial systems or coping with sensory overload during financial tasks. However, with the right strategies and tools, you can develop a solid foundation for financial stability and independence.

One of the first steps in managing finances is understanding your financial situation. This involves tracking your income, expenses, and any existing debts. Creating a detailed overview of your financial landscape can help you identify areas where you may need to make adjustments or seek additional support. Tools such as budgeting apps or financial management software can simplify this process, offering visual representations of your financial data and helping you stay organized.

Budgeting is a critical aspect of financial management. It involves creating a plan for how you will allocate your income to cover various expenses, including necessities like housing and groceries, as well as discretionary spending and savings. Developing a budget requires you to categorize your expenses and set limits for each category. For instance, you might allocate a specific amount for rent, utilities, and groceries, while setting aside funds for savings and occasional splurges.

To manage finances effectively, it's important to establish a routine for reviewing and updating your budget. Regularly tracking your spending and comparing it to your budget can help you identify any discrepancies and make necessary adjustments. Additionally, setting financial goals, such as saving for a vacation or paying off debt, can provide motivation and a clear direction for your financial planning.

Creating a financial plan tailored to your needs can also involve setting up systems to manage bills and payments. Automating payments for recurring expenses, such as utilities or credit card bills, can help ensure that you never miss a due date and avoid late fees. For those who find it challenging to manage multiple deadlines, setting reminders or using a calendar app to track payment dates can be helpful.

Budgeting and Financial Organization Tips

Effective budgeting and financial organization are essential for maintaining control over your finances and achieving your financial goals. As an autistic adult woman, you may have specific preferences or needs that can influence how you approach budgeting and financial organization. Tailoring these strategies to your individual circumstances can make the process more manageable and less overwhelming.

Start by creating a budget that reflects your income and expenses. Categorize your spending into fixed costs, such as rent or mortgage payments, and variable costs, such as groceries or entertainment. This categorization helps you understand where your money is going and identify areas where you might be able to cut back. Using a budgeting app or spreadsheet can make this process easier by providing visual tools to track your income and expenses.

Consider using the envelope system for managing variable expenses. This method involves allocating a specific amount of cash to different spending categories, such as dining out or shopping, and keeping the cash in separate envelopes. When the cash in an envelope runs out, you know you've reached your limit for that category. This approach can be particularly useful for those who prefer a tangible, visual method of budgeting.

Another useful strategy is the 50/30/20 rule, which divides your income into three categories: 50% for needs (e.g., rent, utilities), 30% for wants (e.g., dining out, entertainment), and 20% for savings and debt repayment. This rule provides a straightforward framework for managing your finances and ensuring that you allocate funds appropriately across different areas.

To stay organized, create a system for tracking your financial documents and records. This can include digital storage solutions, such as cloud-based folders, or physical filing systems. Keeping track of receipts, bank statements, and tax documents helps you stay organized and prepared for any financial tasks or audits that may arise.

Regularly reviewing and adjusting your budget is key to maintaining financial stability. Set aside time each month to review your spending, assess whether you're meeting your financial goals, and make any necessary changes to your budget. This practice helps you stay on top of your finances and adapt to any changes in your income or expenses.

Planning for the Future: Savings and Investments

Planning for the future involves setting aside funds for both short-term and long-term goals. For autistic adult women, creating a savings and investment strategy that aligns with your financial goals and risk tolerance is essential for achieving financial independence and security.

Begin by establishing an emergency fund. This fund is designed to cover unexpected expenses, such as medical bills or car repairs, and should ideally contain three to six months' worth of living expenses. Having an emergency fund provides a financial safety net and reduces the stress associated with unforeseen costs.

Once you have an emergency fund in place, consider setting savings goals for specific objectives, such as buying a home, going on vacation, or furthering your education. Define these goals clearly and determine how much money you need to save to achieve them. Break down your savings goals into smaller, manageable amounts and set up automatic transfers to a dedicated savings account to make consistent progress.

Investing is another crucial aspect of financial planning. While it involves higher risks than savings, it also offers the potential for greater returns. When investing, it's important to assess your risk tolerance and investment goals.

Different types of investments, such as stocks, bonds, and mutual funds, have varying levels of risk and potential returns. Researching these options and consulting with a financial advisor can help you make informed decisions.

Consider contributing to retirement accounts, such as an Individual Retirement Account (IRA) or a 401(k). These accounts offer tax advantages and help you build a retirement savings fund. Many employers offer matching contributions for 401(k) plans, which can significantly boost your savings over time. If your employer offers this benefit, try to contribute enough to take full advantage of the match.

Additionally, diversifying your investments can help manage risk and improve your chances of achieving your financial goals. Diversification involves spreading your investments across different asset classes and sectors to reduce the impact of any single investment's poor performance. A well-diversified portfolio can provide more stability and growth potential over the long term.

Navigating Government and Social Support Systems

Navigating government and social support systems can be an essential part of managing your finances and ensuring access to necessary resources. For autistic adult women, understanding the available support options and how to access them can provide valuable assistance in achieving financial stability and independence.

Begin by familiarizing yourself with government programs and benefits that may be available to you. These programs can include Social Security Disability

Insurance (SSDI), Supplemental Security Income (SSI), and Medicaid. Each program has specific eligibility requirements and application processes, so it's important to research these details and determine which programs you may qualify for.

Social Security Disability Insurance (SSDI) provides financial assistance to individuals who are unable to work due to a disability. If you have a documented disability and meet the work history requirements, you may be eligible for SSDI benefits. Applying for SSDI involves providing medical documentation and undergoing a review process to assess your eligibility.

Supplemental Security Income (SSI) offers financial support to individuals with low income and limited resources who are disabled, elderly, or blind. SSI benefits are based on financial need rather than work history, making it a potential option for those with limited income or assets. Similar to SSDI, the application process for SSI involves providing documentation of your financial situation and disability status.

Medicaid is a health insurance program for individuals with low income and limited resources. It provides coverage for a range of medical services, including doctor visits, hospital stays, and prescription medications. Eligibility for Medicaid varies by state, so it's important to check the specific requirements and application process in your area.

In addition to government programs, explore community resources and support organizations that offer financial assistance, advocacy, and other services. Local nonprofits, advocacy groups, and community centers may provide resources such as financial counseling, legal assistance, or assistance with navigating benefits and support systems.

Applying for and managing government benefits can be complex and time-consuming. Seeking assistance from a financial advisor, social worker, or benefits counselor can help you navigate the process and ensure that you access the support you need. These professionals can provide guidance on completing applications, understanding eligibility requirements, and managing benefits effectively.

CHAPTER 10

HEALTH AND WELLNESS

Physical Health and Autism

Physical health is a vital aspect of overall well-being, but it can be especially complex for autistic adult women. Understanding the unique ways autism can impact your physical health is essential in managing and maintaining a healthy lifestyle.

Autism can influence physical health in various ways, one of the most significant being sensory processing differences. These differences can affect how you perceive physical sensations like pain, temperature, and touch. For example, you might have a high pain threshold, which could lead to underreporting or ignoring symptoms that should be addressed. Conversely, you might experience heightened sensitivity, making everyday physical sensations uncomfortable or even painful. These sensory experiences can complicate how you manage your health, as traditional medical advice or treatments may not always align with your sensory needs.

Chronic health conditions are another area where autistic women may face additional challenges. Research has shown that autistic individuals are more likely to experience gastrointestinal issues, sleep disorders, and autoimmune conditions. The exact reasons for these increased risks are still being studied, but they may relate to how autism affects the body's stress response and immune system. For example, if you have gastrointestinal issues, it might be due to food sensitivities that are more common among autistic people. Understanding these connections can help you seek appropriate medical advice and make informed decisions about your health care.

Routine medical care is critical for maintaining good health, but visiting healthcare providers can be a source of anxiety for many autistic women. The sensory overload of a clinical environment, combined with the stress of communicating symptoms and concerns, can make doctor visits overwhelming. It might be helpful to prepare for appointments by writing down your symptoms and any questions you have beforehand. This approach can help you feel more in control and ensure that your concerns are addressed during the visit. Additionally, bringing a trusted friend or family member with you can provide emotional support and assist in communicating with healthcare professionals.

It's also important to recognize that many autistic women have faced challenges in the healthcare system, such as being misunderstood or having their symptoms dismissed. These experiences can lead to a reluctance to seek medical help, which can further complicate health issues. Finding a healthcare provider who is knowledgeable about autism and who listens to your concerns is crucial. Don't hesitate to advocate for yourself by asking questions and requesting explanations when something isn't clear. Your health is important, and you deserve to have your concerns taken seriously.

In addition to regular check-ups, consider how your daily habits and routines affect your physical health. A consistent routine that includes time for self-care, exercise, and relaxation can help you manage stress and improve your overall health. This routine can be tailored to fit your unique needs and preferences, making it easier to stick to over time.

Diet, Nutrition, and Exercise

Maintaining a balanced diet and regular exercise routine is important for everyone, but for autistic women, there can be specific challenges that make these aspects of health more complicated. Understanding how your sensory experiences and preferences impact your diet and exercise habits is key to developing a healthy and sustainable lifestyle.

Sensory sensitivities often play a significant role in dietary preferences and eating habits. Certain textures, flavors, or smells might be overwhelming or unpleasant, leading to a restricted diet that could lack essential nutrients. For instance, you might avoid foods with certain textures or only eat foods that feel familiar and safe. While these preferences are entirely valid, they can sometimes lead to nutritional deficiencies if your diet is too limited.

Working with a dietitian who understands autism can help you find ways to broaden your diet in a way that respects your sensory sensitivities. They can suggest gradual changes, like introducing new foods in small, manageable portions or experimenting with different cooking methods to make foods more appealing. For example, if you find raw vegetables too crunchy, you might try steamed or pureed versions that are easier to eat.

Routine is another important factor in how you approach food. Many autistic individuals find comfort in having a consistent eating schedule, which can be beneficial for managing hunger and energy levels. However, it's important to ensure that your routine includes a variety of foods to meet your nutritional needs. Meal planning can be a useful tool in achieving this balance, allowing you to incorporate different foods into your diet while maintaining the structure you prefer.

Exercise is another crucial component of physical health, but finding the right form of physical activity can be challenging for autistic women. You might experience difficulties with motor coordination, or certain forms of exercise might be uncomfortable due to sensory sensitivities. For example, high-impact activities like running might not be enjoyable if you're sensitive to the feeling of your body moving up and down. Similarly, the noise and social aspects of a gym environment might be overwhelming.

The key to maintaining an exercise routine is finding activities that you enjoy and that fit your sensory preferences. This might involve some trial and error, but there are many options to explore. Low-impact activities like swimming, yoga, or walking can be gentle on your body and provide a calming environment. You might also consider activities that can be done at home, such as using exercise videos or apps, which can offer more control over your environment and reduce sensory stress.

It's important to remember that exercise doesn't have to be formal or structured to be beneficial. Activities like gardening, dancing, or even cleaning can provide physical activity in a way that feels natural and enjoyable. The goal is to stay active in a way that suits your lifestyle and preferences.

Finally, both diet and exercise routines should be flexible enough to accommodate your changing needs and energy levels. If you're having a day when you're feeling particularly sensitive or overwhelmed, it's okay to adjust your routine or take a break. The most important thing is to find a balance that supports your overall well-being and feels sustainable in the long term.

Navigating the Healthcare System

Navigating the healthcare system can be a complex and overwhelming experience, especially for autistic women. The combination of sensory sensitivities, communication challenges, and the need for individualized care can make accessing the medical support you need difficult. However, with the right strategies and support, you can navigate the system more effectively and advocate for your health.

One of the first steps in navigating the healthcare system is finding a provider who understands autism and is willing to work with you to address your specific needs. This might involve doing some research to find a provider who has experience working with autistic patients or who is open to learning about how autism affects your health. When searching for a provider, it's important to ask questions about their experience with autism and their approach to patient care. Finding the right fit can make a significant difference in your healthcare experience, so don't hesitate to take your time in this process.

Once you've found a provider, communication is key to getting the care you need. Before your appointment, take some time to prepare by writing down any symptoms, concerns, or questions you have. This preparation can help you feel more organized and ensure that you don't forget to mention anything important during your visit. If you find it difficult to communicate verbally, consider bringing a written summary of your concerns to give to your provider. This can help ensure that your needs are clearly understood, even if speaking about them is challenging.

Sensory sensitivities can also make healthcare visits challenging. The clinical environment—bright lights, strong smells, and unfamiliar sounds—can be overwhelming and stressful. If you find these aspects of the environment uncomfortable, consider bringing items that can help you manage your sensory sensitivities, such as noise-canceling headphones, sunglasses, or a comforting object. It's also helpful to communicate your sensory needs to the healthcare staff so they can make accommodations where possible. For example, you might ask to wait in a quieter area or request that certain procedures be explained to you in detail before they're performed.

Advocating for your health is another important aspect of navigating the healthcare system. If you feel that your concerns are not being taken seriously or that your needs are not being met, it's important to speak up. This might involve asking for additional tests, seeking a second opinion, or requesting accommodations that can make your healthcare experience more comfortable. Remember, you have the right to receive care that meets your needs and respects your experiences.

Understanding your rights as a patient is also crucial. For example, under laws like the Americans with Disabilities Act (ADA), you have the right to request reasonable accommodations in healthcare settings. This could include things like extended appointment times, adjustments to the clinical environment, or the use of alternative communication methods.

Knowing your rights can empower you to advocate for the care you deserve and ensure that your healthcare experience is as positive and supportive as possible.

In some cases, it might be helpful to have a healthcare advocate or a trusted friend or family member accompany you to appointments. They can help you communicate with your provider, remember important information, and provide emotional support. Having someone with you can also help reduce the anxiety that often accompanies healthcare visits.

Reproductive Health and Hormonal Considerations

Reproductive health is a crucial aspect of overall wellness, encompassing a wide range of topics such as menstruation, contraception, pregnancy, and menopause. For autistic adult women, these areas may require special consideration due to sensory sensitivities, communication challenges, and the need for individualized care.

Menstruation, for example, can be a particularly challenging experience for many autistic women due to sensory sensitivities. The physical sensations associated with menstruation—such as cramps, bloating, and the feeling of menstrual products—can be uncomfortable or even distressing. It's important to find menstrual products that are comfortable for you, whether that means experimenting with different types of pads, tampons, or menstrual cups. You might also find it helpful to track your menstrual cycle so that you can anticipate and prepare for your period each month. This preparation can reduce anxiety and help you manage symptoms more effectively.

When it comes to contraception, there are many options available, and it's important to choose the one that best suits your needs and lifestyle. Some forms of contraception, such as hormonal birth control, can affect your mood or sensory sensitivities, so it's important to discuss these potential side effects with your healthcare provider. They can help you find the right option that aligns with your body's unique responses. For example, if hormonal birth control exacerbates sensory sensitivities or causes mood fluctuations, non-hormonal options like the copper IUD or barrier methods may be more suitable. Understanding your preferences and discussing them openly with your healthcare provider is essential in making an informed decision that prioritizes both your physical and mental well-being.

Pregnancy is another area where autistic women may have specific concerns. The physical and emotional demands of pregnancy, combined with the need to navigate a healthcare system that may not always understand your needs, can be overwhelming. It's crucial to seek out a healthcare team that is supportive, knowledgeable about autism, and willing to accommodate your needs. This might include discussing your sensory preferences for prenatal visits, labor, and delivery, as well as creating a birth plan that takes into account your comfort and anxiety levels.

During pregnancy, you might experience heightened sensory sensitivities or changes in how you process sensory information. For instance, smells might become more intense, or you may become more sensitive to touch. Understanding these changes and preparing for them can help you manage your pregnancy more effectively. It's also important to communicate any concerns or challenges with your healthcare provider so they can offer support and solutions tailored to your needs.

Postpartum care is another critical aspect of reproductive health. After childbirth, many women experience significant hormonal changes that can impact mood, energy levels, and overall well-being. For autistic women, the postpartum period can also bring unique challenges, such as managing sensory overload while caring for a newborn or coping with changes in routine. Having a strong support system in place, whether it's family, friends, or a healthcare team, can make a significant difference in navigating this transition.

Menopause, like menstruation and pregnancy, can also present specific challenges for autistic women. The hormonal changes that occur during menopause can affect mood, sleep, and sensory processing. You might notice increased anxiety, irritability, or changes in how you experience physical sensations. It's important to be aware of these potential changes and to seek support from healthcare providers who can help you manage symptoms effectively. For example, hormone replacement therapy (HRT) might be an option to consider if menopausal symptoms are particularly challenging, but it's essential to discuss the risks and benefits with your healthcare provider.

In addition to the physical changes associated with menopause, the emotional and psychological impact should not be overlooked. Menopause can bring about feelings of loss or confusion as you navigate this new stage of life. Support groups, counseling, or therapy can provide valuable emotional support and help you process these changes in a way that feels manageable and affirming.

Throughout your reproductive health journey, it's essential to prioritize self-care and listen to your body's signals. This might mean taking extra time to rest, seeking out calming activities, or finding ways to reduce stress during particularly challenging times. Remember that your experiences are valid, and it's okay to ask for help when you need it.

Ultimately, reproductive health is a deeply personal aspect of your overall well-being, and it's important to approach it with the same level of care and consideration that you would any other aspect of your health. By understanding your unique needs and advocating for the support you deserve, you can navigate the complexities of reproductive health with confidence and empowerment.

CHAPTER 11

COMMUNITY AND ADVOCACY

Finding Your Tribe: Connecting with the Autism Community

Connecting with a community that understands and accepts you for who you are is vital, especially when navigating the complexities of life as an autistic adult woman. The autism community, with its diverse and supportive environment, offers a place where you can share experiences, learn from others, and find a sense of belonging. Whether you're newly diagnosed or have known about your autism for years, the sense of connection you can gain from being part of this community is invaluable.

One of the most empowering aspects of finding your tribe within the autism community is the realization that you are not alone. Many women, particularly those diagnosed later in life, have felt isolated or misunderstood for much of their lives. They may have struggled with social expectations, communication challenges, or sensory sensitivities without fully understanding why they felt different. Joining a community of others who share similar experiences can be a profound and affirming experience. It's where you can finally exhale, knowing you're surrounded by people who get it—people who understand the nuances of your experiences without you needing to explain every detail.

The autism community is incredibly diverse, encompassing individuals from all walks of life, each with their own unique experiences and perspectives.

This diversity is one of its greatest strengths, as it allows for a rich exchange of ideas and support. Whether through online forums, local support groups, or social media networks, there are countless ways to connect with others who share your journey. These connections can provide not only practical advice and support but also emotional validation and encouragement.

For many autistic women, the online community offers a particularly accessible way to connect with others. Social media platforms, blogs, and forums provide spaces where you can engage at your own pace, read and reflect before responding, and participate in discussions that are meaningful to you. These online spaces can be especially beneficial if you struggle with face-to-face social interactions or if you live in an area with limited in-person resources. Online communities can also offer a sense of global connection, allowing you to learn from and interact with autistic individuals from around the world, broadening your understanding of autism and how it manifests in different cultural contexts.

In addition to finding support and understanding, connecting with the autism community can also open up opportunities for personal growth and learning. Engaging with others who share your experiences can expose you to new perspectives, coping strategies, and resources that you might not have encountered otherwise. Whether it's learning about new sensory tools, discovering a podcast that resonates with your experiences, or finding a book written by another autistic woman, these connections can enrich your life in countless ways.

However, finding your tribe isn't just about receiving support—it's also about giving back. As you become more comfortable within the community, you might find that you have insights, experiences, or skills that can help others. Whether it's offering advice to someone newly diagnosed, sharing your story to inspire others, or simply being a listening ear, your contributions can have a meaningful impact. This reciprocal support is a cornerstone of the autism community, fostering a sense of solidarity and mutual respect.

In essence, finding your tribe within the autism community is about discovering a place where you can be your authentic self, without fear of judgment or misunderstanding. It's about connecting with others who see and appreciate you for who you are, and who can offer the support, understanding, and camaraderie you need to thrive. Whether online or in person, these connections can be a lifeline, providing the strength and encouragement you need to navigate life's challenges with confidence and resilience.

Becoming an Advocate for Yourself and Others

Advocacy is a powerful tool for empowerment, both for yourself and for the broader autistic community. As an autistic woman, becoming an advocate means taking an active role in shaping how autism is understood, discussed, and accommodated in society. It's about using your voice to challenge stereotypes, push for inclusion, and ensure that autistic voices—especially those of women—are heard and respected.

Self-advocacy is often the first step in this journey. It begins with recognizing your own needs, preferences, and rights, and then confidently communicating these to others. This might involve advocating for accommodations at work or school, such as requesting a quiet workspace or asking for written instructions instead of verbal ones. It could also mean educating friends and family about your sensory sensitivities or explaining why certain social situations are challenging for you. Self-advocacy is about standing up for yourself in a way that honors your experiences and ensures that you can navigate the world in a way that feels safe and supportive.

Effective self-advocacy requires a clear understanding of your rights. For example, in the workplace, you have the right to reasonable accommodations under laws like the Americans with Disabilities Act (ADA) in the United States. Knowing these rights empowers you to request the support you need without feeling like you're asking for special treatment. Instead, you're ensuring that you have the tools and environment necessary to succeed, just like anyone else.

Beyond advocating for yourself, many autistic women find a sense of purpose in advocating for others. This might involve participating in local or national autism advocacy organizations, where you can work to raise awareness, influence policy, and promote inclusion. By sharing your experiences and insights, you can help shape a more inclusive society that understands and respects the diverse ways in which autism manifests.

Advocating for others can take many forms. It might involve speaking out against harmful stereotypes or misinformation about autism, challenging practices that exclude or marginalize autistic individuals, or pushing for changes in how autism is diagnosed and treated. For example, many autistic women have been misdiagnosed or undiagnosed for years due to gender biases in the diagnostic process. Advocating for more accurate and inclusive diagnostic criteria is one way to address this issue and ensure that more women receive the support they need.

Another powerful way to advocate for others is through mentorship. As someone who has navigated the challenges of being an autistic woman, you have valuable insights and experiences that can benefit others who are just beginning their journey. Whether through formal mentorship programs or informal connections within the autism community, you can offer guidance, support, and encouragement to those who may be struggling with similar challenges. By sharing your story and offering practical advice, you can help others feel less alone and more empowered to advocate for themselves.

Advocacy is also about raising awareness and promoting understanding. This can involve public speaking, writing articles or blogs, participating in panel discussions, or even engaging in conversations with people in your community. The goal is to educate others about autism, challenge misconceptions, and promote a more inclusive society. By sharing your perspective, you can help others understand that autism is not something to be feared or pitied, but a different way of experiencing the world that deserves respect and accommodation.

Ultimately, becoming an advocate—whether for yourself or others—is about taking control of your narrative and using your experiences to make a positive impact. It's about ensuring that your voice, and the voices of other autistic women, are heard loud and clear. Advocacy is a powerful way to effect change, both in your own life and in the broader world, creating a more inclusive and supportive environment for all autistic individuals.

Raising Awareness and Promoting Inclusion

Raising awareness about autism is a critical aspect of advocacy that can lead to greater understanding, acceptance, and inclusion. For many autistic women, raising awareness is not just about educating others but also about changing the narrative around autism from one of deficit and disorder to one of diversity and strength. By sharing your experiences and educating others, you can help shift perceptions and promote a more inclusive society where autistic individuals are valued for their unique contributions.

One of the key challenges in raising awareness is combating the pervasive myths and misconceptions about autism. Many people still hold outdated or inaccurate views about what autism is and what it means to be autistic. For example, there is a common misconception that all autistic individuals are socially withdrawn or lack empathy, when in reality, many autistic people experience deep emotions and care deeply about others. By addressing these misconceptions head-on, you can help others see autism in a more nuanced and accurate light.

Promoting inclusion is another vital component of raising awareness. Inclusion goes beyond simply making space for autistic individuals; it's about creating environments where autistic people can thrive. This might involve advocating for sensory-friendly spaces, promoting the use of clear and direct communication, or encouraging the adoption of flexible work policies that accommodate different needs. Inclusion also means ensuring that autistic voices are represented in discussions and decision-making processes that affect the autistic community.

One effective way to raise awareness and promote inclusion is through storytelling. By sharing your personal experiences as an autistic woman, you can help others understand the challenges and joys of living with autism. Personal stories have the power to break down barriers, challenge stereotypes, and foster empathy. When people hear about the real-life experiences of autistic individuals, they are more likely to see beyond the label of autism and appreciate the person behind it.

Another important aspect of raising awareness is advocating for systemic change. This might involve pushing for changes in how autism is diagnosed and treated, advocating for better support services, or promoting policies that ensure equal opportunities for autistic individuals in education, employment, and healthcare. By working to change the systems that affect autistic people, you can help create a society that is more inclusive and supportive of neurodiversity.

Collaboration is also key to raising awareness and promoting inclusion. Working with other autistic individuals, advocacy organizations, and allies can amplify your efforts and lead to greater impact. Whether through joint campaigns, community events, or collaborative projects, working together can help you reach a wider audience and create lasting change.

Finally, it's important to remember that raising awareness is an ongoing process. It's not something that can be achieved overnight, but rather a continuous effort to educate, advocate, and promote understanding. By staying committed to this work, you can help build a world where autistic individuals are respected, valued, and included in all aspects of society.

The Power of Storytelling: Sharing Your Journey

Storytelling is one of the most powerful tools for advocacy and connection. As an autistic woman, sharing your journey can be a transformative experience, both for you and for those who hear your story. It allows you to reclaim your narrative, celebrate your strengths, and provide insight into the unique challenges and triumphs that come with being autistic. Through storytelling, you can break down stereotypes, foster empathy, and inspire others, whether they are autistic or not.

When you share your story, you offer a glimpse into your world—a world that is often misunderstood or misrepresented. For many people, hearing the personal experiences of someone with autism can be a revelation. It can challenge preconceived notions and open their eyes to the reality that autism is not a one-size-fits-all condition. Instead, it's a spectrum of diverse experiences, each shaped by individual personalities, circumstances, and choices.

Your story is a powerful reminder that autistic women, like all people, are multifaceted and complex. You may have faced challenges with sensory sensitivities, social interactions, or communication, but you've also likely developed unique coping strategies, discovered unexpected strengths, and achieved successes that might not fit into the typical narrative of what success looks like. By sharing these experiences, you contribute to a richer, more nuanced understanding of autism.

Moreover, storytelling can be a form of self-advocacy. It's an opportunity to articulate your needs, express your emotions, and assert your identity. In a world that often imposes labels and assumptions on autistic individuals, telling your own story allows you to define yourself on your own terms. It's a way of saying, "This is who I am, and this is what I need," which can be empowering for both you and those who hear your story.

Sharing your journey can also create a sense of connection and community. When you tell your story, others who have had similar experiences may feel a sense of validation and belonging. They might recognize themselves in your words and find comfort in knowing that they are not alone. This can be particularly important for autistic women, who may have felt isolated or misunderstood throughout their lives. By sharing your story, you create a space where others can see themselves reflected and feel a sense of kinship and solidarity.

In addition to connecting with other autistic individuals, storytelling can also educate and inform those who are not on the spectrum. By sharing your experiences, you help others understand what it means to be autistic, how it affects your daily life, and what they can do to be more supportive and inclusive. This can lead to greater empathy and a more inclusive society, where neurodiversity is celebrated rather than stigmatized.

Your story doesn't have to be a grand, sweeping narrative to be impactful. Sometimes, the most powerful stories are those that focus on the small, everyday moments—how you navigate a sensory overload, what it feels like to communicate in a world that often doesn't understand you, or how you've learned to advocate for yourself in a neurotypical environment. These moments can resonate deeply with others and offer a window into the lived experience of autism.

If you're unsure where to start with your storytelling, consider reflecting on the key moments in your life that have shaped who you are today. Think about the challenges you've faced, the strategies you've developed to cope with them, and the successes you've achieved along the way. Your story is uniquely yours, and there is no right or wrong way to tell it. Whether you choose to share it through writing, speaking, art, or any other medium, your voice is valuable and needed.

As you share your journey, it's important to remember that your story is ongoing. Your experiences, perspectives, and insights will continue to evolve, and so will your story. By embracing storytelling as a lifelong practice, you can continue to contribute to the conversation about autism, advocate for yourself and others, and build connections with those who share your journey.

In the end, the power of storytelling lies in its ability to humanize and connect. Your story has the potential to touch hearts, change minds, and inspire action. It's a powerful tool for raising awareness, promoting inclusion, and advocating for a world where autistic individuals are understood, respected, and celebrated. So, don't be afraid to share your journey—your voice is a vital part of the ongoing narrative of autism, and it deserves to be heard.

CHAPTER 12

NAVIGATING MAJOR LIFE TRANSITIONS

Major life transitions can be challenging for anyone, but for autistic women, these changes often come with unique difficulties that require careful consideration and planning. Whether it's moving out and living independently, navigating marriage, divorce, and relationship changes, aging with autism, or coping with grief and loss, these experiences can be overwhelming. However, with the right support and strategies, it is possible to navigate these transitions in a way that respects your needs and promotes your well-being.

Moving Out and Living Independently

Moving out and living independently is a significant milestone in any adult's life, but it can be particularly daunting for autistic women. The thought of managing daily tasks, handling finances, and dealing with the unpredictability of life can be overwhelming. However, with the right preparation and support, independent living can be a rewarding and empowering experience.

One of the first steps in moving out is to assess your readiness. This includes understanding your strengths and areas where you might need support. For example, if you struggle with executive functioning tasks like planning, organizing, and time management, it might be helpful to set up systems that can help you stay on track. This could include using apps or planners to keep track of appointments and tasks, setting reminders for important deadlines, and breaking down larger tasks into smaller, more manageable steps.

Another important aspect of independent living is financial management. This includes budgeting, paying bills, and managing expenses. It's important to create a budget that reflects your income and expenses, ensuring that you have enough to cover your needs while also saving for the future. If you're not confident in your financial skills, consider seeking out resources or support, such as financial literacy programs or working with a financial advisor who understands autism.

Living independently also means taking care of your living space. This includes cleaning, cooking, and maintaining your home. If these tasks feel overwhelming, it might be helpful to create a routine or schedule that breaks down these tasks into smaller, more manageable parts. For example, you might designate certain days for specific chores or prepare meals in advance to make cooking easier. If sensory sensitivities make certain tasks difficult, consider finding alternatives that work better for you, such as using cleaning products that are less harsh or finding recipes that are simple and easy to follow.

Social support is also crucial when living independently. Whether it's friends, family, or a support network, having people you can rely on for help or companionship can make a big difference. Don't be afraid to ask for help when you need it, whether it's with practical tasks or just someone to talk to when you're feeling overwhelmed. There are also many online communities and support groups for autistic women that can provide a sense of connection and understanding.

Ultimately, moving out and living independently is about finding what works best for you. It's okay to take things one step at a time and to seek out support when you need it. With the right preparation and resources, independent living can be a positive and empowering experience that allows you to take control of your life and live in a way that feels true to you.

Marriage, Divorce, and Relationship Changes

Navigating relationships is a complex and often challenging aspect of life, and this is particularly true for autistic women. Whether it's marriage, divorce, or other relationship changes, these transitions can bring about a range of emotions and challenges that require careful navigation.

Marriage can be a deeply fulfilling experience, but it also requires a great deal of communication, compromise, and understanding. For autistic women, sensory sensitivities, communication differences, and social challenges can sometimes make marriage more complex. It's important to have open and honest communication with your partner about your needs, boundaries, and expectations. This includes discussing topics such as sensory sensitivities, social preferences, and communication styles. For example, you might need to establish clear routines or use specific communication strategies that work for both you and your partner.

It's also important to recognize that marriage, like any relationship, requires effort from both partners. This means being willing to work through challenges together, seek out support when needed, and continue to learn and grow as a couple. There may be times when you need to seek out counseling or therapy, either individually or as a couple, to help navigate challenges and strengthen your relationship.

Unfortunately, not all marriages last, and divorce or separation can be a difficult and painful experience. For autistic women, the emotional toll of divorce can be particularly intense, especially if the relationship provided a sense of stability and routine. It's important to give yourself time to grieve and process the emotions that come with the end of a relationship. This might include seeking out therapy or counseling to help you navigate the emotional challenges of divorce.

During this time, it's also important to take care of yourself and establish a new routine that works for you. This might include finding new social supports, engaging in self-care activities, and exploring new interests or hobbies. It's okay to take things one step at a time and to seek out support when you need it.

Relationship changes can also include the loss of friendships or shifts in social dynamics. It's important to remember that relationships, whether romantic or platonic, are a two-way street, and it's okay to set boundaries and prioritize your well-being. If a relationship is no longer serving you or is causing you harm, it's okay to step back or end the relationship. At the same time, it's important to seek out new connections and to be open to the possibility of forming new relationships that are supportive and fulfilling.

Ultimately, navigating relationships is about finding what works best for you and your needs. Whether it's marriage, divorce, or other relationship changes, it's important to approach these transitions with self-compassion and to seek out support when needed. With the right resources and strategies, it's possible to navigate these changes in a way that promotes your well-being and allows you to build healthy, fulfilling relationships.

Aging with Autism: Preparing for the Future

Aging is a natural part of life, and for autistic women, it comes with its own unique challenges and considerations. As you age, it's important to think about your future and to take steps to ensure that you are prepared for the changes that come with aging.

One of the first steps in preparing for the future is to think about your long-term needs and goals. This includes considering your health, living arrangements, and financial situation. As you age, you may need to make adjustments to your lifestyle or seek out additional support to ensure that you can continue to live independently and maintain your well-being.

It's also important to think about your healthcare needs as you age. This might include finding healthcare providers who understand autism and can provide the care you need. As you age, you may also need to consider issues such as mobility, sensory sensitivities, and other health concerns that may arise. It's important to have open and honest communication with your healthcare providers about your needs and to advocate for the care that is right for you.

Another important aspect of aging with autism is thinking about your living arrangements. This might include considering whether you want to continue living independently, move in with family, or explore other housing options such as assisted living or a retirement community. It's important to think about what living situation will best meet your needs and to plan accordingly.

Financial planning is also crucial as you age. This includes thinking about your income, savings, and any financial support you may need in the future. It's important to create a financial plan that reflects your long-term goals and ensures that you have the resources you need to live comfortably as you age. This might include working with a financial advisor or seeking out resources that can help you plan for your future.

Social support is also important as you age. This might include maintaining connections with friends and family, seeking out new social opportunities, and staying engaged in activities that bring you joy and fulfillment. It's important to continue to build and maintain a support network that can provide companionship and assistance as you age.

Ultimately, aging with autism is about finding what works best for you and your needs. It's important to approach aging with a sense of self-compassion and to seek out support when needed. With the right resources and strategies, it's possible to navigate the challenges of aging in a way that promotes your well-being and allows you to continue living a fulfilling life.

Coping with Grief and Loss

Grief and loss are inevitable parts of life, and they can be particularly challenging for autistic women. Whether it's the loss of a loved one, the end of a relationship, or other significant life changes, grief can bring about a range of emotions that can be difficult to navigate.

One of the first steps in coping with grief is to allow yourself to feel and process your emotions. Grief is a deeply personal experience, and there is no right or wrong way to grieve. It's important to give yourself permission to feel whatever emotions come up, whether it's sadness, anger, confusion, or even relief. It's also important to recognize that grief is not a linear process, and you may experience a range of emotions at different times.

It can be helpful to find ways to express and process your grief. This might include talking to a trusted friend or therapist, journaling, or engaging in creative activities such as art or music. Finding ways to express your emotions can help you process your grief and begin to heal.

Social support is also crucial when coping with grief. It's important to reach out to others for support, whether it's friends, family, or a support group. Talking to others who have experienced similar losses can provide comfort and validation, and it can help you feel less alone in your grief.

Self-care is also important during times of grief. It's important to take care of your physical, emotional, and mental well-being. This might include engaging in activities that bring you comfort, such as spending time in nature, practicing mindfulness, or engaging in hobbies that bring you joy. It's also important to prioritize rest and relaxation, as grief can be physically and emotionally exhausting.

It's also important to recognize that grief doesn't have a set timeline, and healing is a process that takes time. You may find that certain anniversaries, holidays, or other reminders can trigger feelings of grief even long after the loss has occurred. It's okay to revisit these emotions and to give yourself the space and time to process them as they arise. Be gentle with yourself and understand that healing is not about "getting over" the loss, but rather learning to live with it in a way that honors your experience and your feelings.

If you find that grief becomes overwhelming or starts to interfere with your ability to function in daily life, it may be helpful to seek professional support. Grief counseling or therapy can provide a safe space to explore your emotions and to develop coping strategies that work for you. A therapist with experience in working with autistic clients can also help you navigate any sensory sensitivities or communication challenges that may arise as part of your grief process.

Finally, remember that it's okay to seek joy and fulfillment even in the midst of grief. Engaging in activities that bring you a sense of peace or connection can be an important part of healing. Whether it's spending time with loved ones, pursuing a passion project, or simply finding moments of calm in your day, these small acts of self-care can help you find balance as you navigate the complexities of grief.

Navigating major life transitions is challenging for anyone, but for autistic women, these experiences can be particularly complex. However, with the right support, strategies, and resources, it's possible to approach these transitions in a way that honors your needs and promotes your well-being. Whether you're moving out and living independently, navigating relationships, preparing for the future as you age, or coping with grief and loss, it's important to remember that you are not alone. By seeking out the support you need, being gentle with yourself, and embracing the unique aspects of your journey, you can navigate these transitions with resilience and strength.

Your experiences are valid, and your path is your own. No matter what challenges or changes you face, know that you have the ability to navigate them in a way that aligns with who you are and what you need. Take things one step at a time, seek out the resources and support that resonate with you, and remember that your well-being is always worth prioritizing. With the right approach, you can move through life's transitions with confidence and grace, creating a life that reflects your unique strengths and values. and empowered life involves embracing change and growth. Life is full of transitions and challenges, and your journey will inevitably involve moments of uncertainty or difficulty. However, these moments are also opportunities for growth and self-discovery. By approaching change with an open mind and a willingness to learn, you can turn challenges into stepping stones that lead you closer to the life you envision for yourself.

A key aspect of living a fulfilling life is also learning to balance different aspects of your life—work, relationships, personal time, and self-care. For autistic women, this balance might look different than it does for others, and that's okay. It's important to find a rhythm that works for you, one that allows you to meet your responsibilities while also making time for the things that nourish your soul. This might mean setting boundaries with work, carving out time for hobbies or rest, or creating routines that help you feel grounded and in control.

Furthermore, a fulfilling and empowered life is one where you feel confident in your identity and your place in the world. This confidence comes from self-acceptance—recognizing that you are enough just as you are, and that your worth is not determined by how well you fit into societal expectations. It's about owning your story, with all its complexities and nuances, and being proud of who you are and what you've accomplished.

Living a fulfilling and empowered life also means being an advocate for yourself and others. By sharing your experiences and insights, you can help raise awareness and promote understanding of the unique challenges and strengths of autistic women. Advocacy can take many forms, from speaking out about issues that matter to you, to supporting others in their journeys, to simply living your life in a way that challenges stereotypes and misconceptions. Your voice is powerful, and by using it, you can make a positive impact on the world around you.

Finally, living a fulfilling and empowered life is about joy and fulfillment, but it's also about resilience and persistence. Life will undoubtedly present you with obstacles, and there will be times when things don't go as planned. However, by staying true to your values, nurturing your passions, and remaining connected to your sense of purpose, you can navigate these challenges with strength and grace. Remember, thriving is not about having a perfect life; it's about finding meaning, joy, and empowerment in the life you have, and continually striving to make it the best it can be.

CONCLUSION

Conclusion

Embracing Your Unique Journey

As we reach the end of this book, it's important to reflect on the uniqueness of your journey. Living as an autistic woman in a world that often misunderstands or underestimates you can be challenging, but it's also filled with opportunities for growth, discovery, and empowerment. Your path may not look like anyone else's, and that's okay. In fact, it's more than okay—it's wonderful.

Every experience you've had, every hurdle you've overcome, and every triumph you've celebrated has contributed to making you who you are today. Embracing your unique journey means acknowledging your strengths and accepting your differences without apology. It means letting go of the pressure to conform to neurotypical standards and instead recognizing that your perspective and way of being are valuable.

Your journey is shaped by your personal experiences, and while others might not always understand your choices or struggles, that doesn't make them any less valid. It's okay to take time to find your rhythm and decide what works best for you. Maybe you thrive in solitude, or perhaps you find joy in connecting deeply with a few trusted friends. Maybe you're still figuring out what environments make you feel most comfortable and productive, or you've discovered that a structured routine brings you peace. Whatever your path, remember it is yours to define.

You have the right to explore who you are without judgment. This means allowing yourself to try new things, to fail and learn, and to redefine success on your own terms. It means recognizing that it's okay to prioritize your needs, even when others might not understand why certain things are necessary for you. It also means being gentle with yourself on the hard days, when everything feels overwhelming, and remembering that those days don't define you.

It's easy to get caught up in comparisons, to feel like you should be doing more or doing things differently. But embracing your unique journey means recognizing that you are enough just as you are. The world may not always be kind or accommodating, but you have the power to carve out spaces that honor your true self. You have the right to advocate for your needs, to set boundaries that protect your well-being, and to seek out environments that celebrate your strengths.

Know that every step you take, no matter how small, is part of a larger journey toward self-acceptance and growth. There is no rush, no deadline, and no one path to follow. You are allowed to make mistakes, to change your mind, and to grow at your own pace. Your journey is unique, and that is its greatest strength.

Continuing the Conversation

The conversation about autism in adult women is still just beginning. For far too long, autistic women have been marginalized, their experiences overlooked or misunderstood. But that is changing, and you are a vital part of that change. By sharing your experiences, speaking up, and connecting with others, you are helping to create a more inclusive and understanding world.

Continuing the conversation means staying engaged and connected, even when it feels uncomfortable or challenging. It means being willing to share your story, to listen to others, and to advocate for change. It means recognizing that your voice matters—that every time you speak up, you make it easier for someone else to do the same.

This book is just one piece of the puzzle. There are many voices out there, and each one adds something valuable to the conversation. As you continue on your journey, I encourage you to seek out other perspectives, to connect with the broader autism community, and to find the spaces where you feel heard and understood. Whether through online communities, local support groups, or even just one-on-one conversations, building connections with others who share your experiences can be incredibly powerful.

Don't be afraid to challenge misconceptions or stereotypes about autism. The more we talk about the diverse ways autism can manifest, the better we can educate others and foster understanding. Be open to learning from others, too—there is always something new to discover, and each person's experience offers a different lens through which to view the world.

Remember, the conversation doesn't have to be formal or structured. It can happen in everyday moments, through small acts of advocacy, or simply by being your authentic self. Every time you share a piece of your story, educate a friend, or correct a misunderstanding, you are contributing to a larger movement toward acceptance and understanding.

Continuing the conversation also means being open to growth and change within yourself. As you learn more about autism and about yourself, your understanding may evolve. Be willing to embrace that evolution, to challenge your own assumptions, and to continue seeking knowledge and connection. You are a lifelong learner, and every new piece of information or insight can help you navigate the world in a way that feels right for you.

....

As we close this book, I want you to know that you are not alone. You are part of a diverse and vibrant community of autistic women who are redefining what it means to be autistic, every single day. You are stronger than you know, and you have already accomplished so much just by being here, by reading these words, and by choosing to learn more about yourself and your needs.

The path ahead may not always be easy, but you are capable of navigating it with grace and resilience. Trust yourself. Trust your instincts, your insights, and your experiences. You have a unique perspective that the world needs, and you have every right to stand tall in your truth.

Don't be afraid to reach out for support when you need it. There is strength in asking for help, in acknowledging when things are hard, and in allowing others to be there for you. Know that there are people out there who understand, who want to support you, and who value your voice and your contributions.

Remember that self-care is not a luxury; it is a necessity. Take time to listen to your body and your mind. Allow yourself moments of rest, reflection, and peace. Self-care can be as simple as finding a quiet place to recharge, immersing yourself in a favorite activity, or surrounding yourself with people who make you feel safe and understood. It might also mean setting boundaries, saying no when something feels overwhelming, and giving yourself permission to prioritize your well-being above all else.